BOOKS BY

William G. Saltonstall

LEWIS PERRY OF EXETER   1980

PORTS OF PISCATAQUA
A MARITIME HISTORY OF NEW HAMPSHIRE   1941

LEWIS PERRY OF EXETER

A GENTLE MEMOIR

LEWIS PERRY
OF EXETER:
A GENTLE MEMOIR

❧

WILLIAM G. SALTONSTALL

Foreword by David McCord

Cop a

ATHENEUM

NEW YORK

1980

Library of Congress Cataloging in Publication Data

Saltonstall, William Gurdon, 1905–
    Lewis Perry of Exeter.

    1. Perry, Lewis, 1877–1970. 2. High school
principals—New Hampshire—Biography. 3. Phillips
Exeter Academy—History. I. Title.
    LD7501.E936P477   1980   373.1'2'0120924 [B]   79-23837
    ISBN 0-689-11056-1

TO KATHIE WITH DELIGHT

The gentleman is learned, and a most rare speaker,
To nature none more bound; his training such
That he may furnish and instruct great teachers
And never seek for aid out of himself.

SHAKESPEARE, *Henry VIII*, I, 2, 111–114

FOREWORD

BY DAVID McCORD

ᴥ᎒Ꭶ᎒ᴧ

B ACK IN THE 1920s I had the more than occasional
privilege of fishing with Ferris Greenslet: first
for trout in New Hampshire's Ammonoosuc, and
later for landlocked salmon in Kennebago Stream far
down in Maine. Ferris was then editor-in-chief of
Houghton Mifflin Company, and could drop a dry fly
into an imaginary thimble as well as—even better
than—could tall Bliss Perry, a distinguished elder
brother of the subject of this book. Ferris gladly
taught me what he could about this abstruse art, and
I as gladly tried to learn. And it was Ferris who used
to say, when I inquired about some bulky typescript
which accompanied him: "I've read every word of
it." I say this now to myself in sadness for having
finished the book you are holding. And I think to
myself: what a long, long time since I have had such
total reading pleasure as it has given me.

A different pleasure, to be sure, from what I remember of my early entrance into the several worlds
of giants such as Dickens, Conrad, Hudson, Borrow,
Mark Twain, Parkman, Joyce; or into that bright

small polished planet of Max Beerbohm. Yet the old essential shiver of anticipation carried me from page to page. I can still feel it in remembrance; for this is an easy, civilized, simple story of a great human being, if not a man of heroic stature. But it will stun you, nonetheless, again and again to face the unspoiled daily grandeur of life used with gusto and met with honest reality. You may not have known Lewis Perry, as I did, for thirty years; you may not have known his biographer, as I have, for fifty. But all the more reason, then, for the sheer enjoyment and surprise ahead of you. I never traveled with Dr. Perry as the reader will. I never saw him at faculty meetings. But I did see and hear him on the platform many times: never for long enough; and never for one moment was I out from under his spell—a protracted spell like that of Rex Harrison's acting in *My Fair Lady*. I do not exaggerate; for to listen to Lewis Perry was something like being inside what the physicists call a force field—all-a-tingle. He had the perfect timing that Olivier has praised in Harrison; he could control the "pregnant caesuras," as Mr. Saltonstall so shrewdly observes; and pregnant caesuras and the use of them are what most speakers fail to organize and understand. I know for a fact that listening to, and watching, Lewis Perry in action truly slowed me down before the lectern or in a classroom. I owe him a debt he never was aware of.

Well, in the weave of the world, to borrow a phrase from Wallace Stevens, a few particular threads will tangle here and there where lives and happenings

cross and touch. Lewis Perry, as a boy, very quickly
dropped out of Andover over a Latin conflict (and
his father's anger at the teacher) and went to Lawrenceville, from which he graduated. My father was
a Lawrenceville graduate; my great uncle was fired
from Andover a century and a half ago, though not, I
think, for ablatives too absolute. (Whistler said, on
being fired from West Point, "If silicon had been a
gas, I'd have been a major general.") Lewis Perry's
son taught at Lawrenceville and was connected with
Dickenson House, of which a cousin of mine was at
one time Master. Carroll Perry, older minister brother,
wrote two books, long a pair of my most treasured
vade mecum: A Professor of Life and *Bill Pratt: the
Sawbuck Philosopher*, referred to in these pages.
Lastly, the one thread which I failed to unravel led
from Johnny Pesky of the Red Sox, and of my Lincoln High School in Portland, Oregon, to Lewis
Perry—not only a tennis champion but a good second
base—who saw Pesky play. I did not.

A lot of laughter is in this book; a lot of aphorisms,
epigrams, wit, and humor are in it. Examples:

One cannot be taught how to teach.
After twenty-two years we (Perry and George B.
Rogers, Williams graduate and senior member
of the Exeter faculty) never had a disagreement,
though we did not always agree.

A warm word is better than a cold medal.

He took life as a long distance runner.

He observed the foibles of peccant man.

Lewis Perry was once kissed by Myra Hess.

I believe in a classical education, an old-fashioned education.

No one was ever a stranger in his (Perry's) presence.

A complete charmer and the greatest bluffer who ever lived.

Dr. Perry's three decades of service to Exeter came at a time when letter writing was still an art; and letters on important matters still held priority over the telephone. Indeed, this book, if one could open every page at once, would look like a long, colorful clothesline with letters (often adroitly excerpted) flying in the breeze. And what fluent, literate letters most of them are! Fine ones from the Perry out-basket; and from the alumni in-basket so many, so succinct and well controlled. After you have read a senior's letter critical of the Harkness Plan, you will not fail to believe that the Exeter English Department is tops in this Johnny-can't-read-write-spell-or-punctuate crazy world of ours. Even that young critic at his typewriter acknowledges the truth of this. He would at sixteen have appreciated the bread and butter letter from a New Hampshire Boston banker in the mid-twenties to a Boston surgeon who had entertained him on the Cape. "Dear Bob: Some parties deserve a letter. Some don't. Yours does. Here's mine."

Wherewith I may conclude these sesame words by quoting in full a brief talk by Lewis Perry, given

at my request in Cambridge in 1952 to the assembled
Class Agents of the Harvard Fund. That it was beautifully delivered and a resounding (and profitable)
success, the follower of the text may easily guess. Just
reading it to myself after twenty-seven years brings
back the genial, kindly, speaker—as much at home as
though he were in Williamstown—with his perfect
timing, willingness to help a friend and a cause all
in one; and above that, the *conviction* of the man.
This talk, save for one brief quotation, is not a part
of Mr. Saltonstall's book. Yet it is, in essence, a
kind of miniature biography; and I think and hope it
will, all by itself, prepare the reader for what lies just
ahead of him. Perhaps I should suggest that the head-
long spirit of the biographer's narrative slacks off
with Dr. Perry's retirement as Principal Instructor in
1946. Of course this is the way of *all* biographies. Only
the autobiographer—Hudson in *Far Away and Long
Ago*, for example—can eliminate the cornhusks and
the dross. "Art is the path of the creator to his work,"
said Emerson. And

> When the mystique dies
> The tributes rise.

Dr. Perry lived on to enjoy the many tributes justly
paid him. A delightful character, as delightful in this
book as out of it, he diminishes and yet is not diminished: see his jovial Jovian remark during the ambulance journey to a nursing home in Bryn Mawr. I
for one (and I would guess for many) would not
have it otherwise.

Saltonstall, of a line of Saltonstall Harvard graduates stretching back to the class of 1642, has made

remarkable use of uncluttered pertinent material. As much at home in a single shell or a sailboat as he was on the hockey rink, he appears to me in the role of attentive biographer who has written this book while sitting in a bouncing dinghy made fast to a trim and seaworthy yawl where all the action is. Not once, with his restraint, does he haul in, climb aboard, give orders, and take over.

What Mother Lives On

By Lewis Perry

I REMEMBER A Sunday School class when I was a small boy where the teacher thought it would be a good thing if we repeated a verse from the Bible or a sentiment as we dropped in our pennies. The first two givers were little girls. One of them said in dropping in her penny: "It is more blessed to give than to receive" and the teacher beamed. The second little girl said sweetly: "Blessed are they that give to the poor." The experiment was certainly a success. The third was a boy, a playmate of mine who remarked rather gruffly: "A fool and his money are soon parted."

We have to deal with the third class, and the most successful Class Agents are those who can bring ungenerous sinners to repentance. This is a job of bringing critics into the eleemosynary fold. I can't tell you how many criticisms I have heard of Harvard and of

Exeter and some even of Deerfield, and the critics and the gossips are the ones we must get.

The gossips are our danger: The men who say, "I will never give a cent as long as so-and-so is teaching." My experience has been that they would never give much anyway, but they constitute a challenge. The truth somehow has a way of emerging eventually! And we believe the truth is on our side.

The times in which we live make our efforts of unusual importance. The novelist Stendhal describes a young man in the Napoleonic wars. He loses three successive horses, he is shunted from one side to the other, he gets in everybody's way. Befuddled with brandy he misses his glimpse of the Emperor; he is wounded while ineffectually striving to stem the rout of the demoralized cavalry across the bridge. Not until the next day when he reaches Amiens and buys a newspaper does he learn the answer to two questions which have been troubling him: Was what he had seen a battle, and was that battle Waterloo?

How like our predicament half way through the 20th century in the thick of tremendous events which we do not more than half understand, if that. Would someone kindly tell us whether this is the death of a world or the birth of a world or both? And what if this should prove to have been one of the great ages of history?

The great ages, Augustan Rome and Elizabethan England, were unstable ages. Harvard is as stable as anything you can find in an imperfect world. She is old as we count things in America. She must be supported. When I was a small boy, in the search of Enlivening Conversation, I was accustomed to frequent on winter days the warm office of the local livery stable run by a great local character named Jim Waterman. Jim was over seventy years old at the time, and one day to my amazement Jim turned a perfect cartwheel. I was speechless, but Jim, as he adjusted his coat, remarked: "Lewis, you can't do that on water." Harvard cannot do what she must do on the income from her endowments. And so the Fund officers and all of you Agents have the delicate and supremely important task of bringing in more money for your Alma Mater. The money which you bring in is what your mother lives on. You are the wage-earners for the family. And you must get this money from those who are made to feel that they should do as much for their College as they do for their Church and their hospital. In a time like this the sights must be lifted, on the part of a greater and greater Harvard, by men who carry Harvard in their hearts, as a man like Allston Burr carried Harvard in his heart. He gave Harvard a day-to-day spiritual and intellectual as well as financial support.

I come back to sentiment and memory—the memory of things big and little which make Harvard what she is.

One of the great givers to Exeter when he was old and ill came back for an Exeter Commencement. He had been a tremendous worker and business adventurer. I suppose most business men who knew him would have called him hard-boiled. He did not attend the Commencement Exercises but stayed in his room in the dormitory for the youngest boys. Somehow he had discovered books he had read as a boy fifty years before, and when I came back to get him, he was reading of all things Scott's *Lady of the Lake*.

James Barrie has said that memory is given to us that we may have roses in December. These roses of yours can make of this 1952 campaign the greatest success which the Harvard Fund has known.

INTRODUCTION

❦

FOUNDED IN 1638, Exeter is a colonial town in southeastern New Hampshire, at the line where the fresh river Squamscott comes down over the falls to meet tidewater. Though the town is only about ten miles direct from Portsmouth and the coast, Exeter's schooners and gundalows once had to navigate perhaps twenty-five miles of curves, bays, and oxbows before they reached the open sea between Portsmouth, New Hampshire and Kittery, Maine. For a time Exeter served as state capitol, and both George Washington and Abraham Lincoln visited and viewed its waterfront, mills, and surrounding farms. Washington, with characteristic understatement, called it "a tolerable town." Lincoln's son was in the academy.

In 1781, when Exeter was 143 years old, one of its leading merchants, John Phillips, founded Phillips Exeter Academy. Three years before he had assisted his nephew Samuel Phillips in founding Phillips Academy, Andover. Both schools were and are private academies dedicated to public service. Both have enjoyed periods of great growth and exultation, and both have endured times of struggle. They have shared an enormous mutual respect, and they have enjoyed an intense but healthy academic and athletic rivalry. Now, as they enter their third centuries, they retain the roots of those Puritan and American virtues upon which they were built.

Phillips Exeter Academy is located near the center of town. At first glance the school appears an awesome conglomeration of classrooms, dormitories, gymnasiums, playing fields, and facilities for art, music, and drama. But in a far more profound sense it is a family: more than 100 faculty, 970 students, some 50 emeriti, more than 350 staff members, and 15,000 alumni, all of whom have worked to reach toward the standards set by John Phillips 200 years ago.

Eleven men have served as principal of Phillips Exeter Academy. This book is the story of one of them, the eighth: Dr. Lewis Perry.

During the years he served Exeter, he became one of the "giants," the great headmasters who led their schools for decades and shaped much of independent secondary education in the twentieth century: Alfred Stearns of Andover, Endicott Peabody of Groton, Frank Boyden of Deerfield, Father Frederick Sill of Kent, Samuel Drury of St. Paul's, to name a few. They were a remarkable group, men of vision and dynamism, who had the capacity to lead and to inspire others to lead after them. Like these other giants, Perry left an enduring mark on his school. Yet even among that singular group Perry was a singular man.

When he assumed the position of principal after the sudden death of Dr. Harlan P. Amen, who had revitalized the school after a dark period in the late nineteenth century, Perry faced a unique challenge. Exeter was like a great, growing child, full of energy and enthusiasm and in need of the freedom to mature, yet in need as well of a tempering, fatherly hand. Lewis Perry became that father: demanding, urging, challenging, yet always guiding with a spirit of humanity and grace.

This book, however, is not strictly about a man and a school, but rather about a man and a way of life. Lewis Perry embodied a tradition and approach to life rare at any time and rarer than ever today. His infallible sense of humor and his delight in music and drama, coupled with his unflagging concern and joy in the intellectual, moral, and physical development of young men, made him loom very large in the lives of thousands—including one young man, who, in 1922, when a senior at Milton Academy, attended a Sunday evening chapel service. I had never seen or heard of Dr. Perry, but after that service I told my parents that I would like to spend a postgraduate year at the school of which he was principal. Perry seemed to be addressing his remarks directly at me, and the combination of warmth and exuberance in his brief words moved me. My parents agreed, and the next year I attended Exeter.

It was the beginning of a friendship that lasted forty-eight years. I was a student under Dr. Perry from 1923 to 1924 and his colleague as a faculty member from 1932 to 1946. In 1946, the year of his retirement as principal, he quietly urged the trustees to consider me for the job. Thus, I became his successor from 1946 to 1963. When at the age of fifty-eight I resigned to direct the Peace Corps in Nigeria, his only comment, at the age of eighty-six, was: "Boys will be boys."

This sketch is a prejudiced view of his life—an affectionate but, I hope, objective effort to share his great qualities and his frailties. Many sang his praise, but he took it with the proverbial grain of salt. "Praise," he was fond of saying, "is all right so long as you don't inhale it."

During his Exeter years and for the rest of his life, my subject was always respectfully known as Dr. Perry. The formality came naturally. He had no earned doctorate, but after he became principal of Exeter in 1914, he was awarded several honorary degrees. Few, if any, of his colleagues on the faculty called him by his first name. In general I shall refer to him as Lewis during his student years, Professor Perry during his teaching period at Williams, and Perry thereafter.

No one has officially asked me to write about him. Some have said that nothing I write can capture his spirit or do him justice, and they may well be correct. In this sense he is beyond biography. But it seems to me worth attempting this gentle memoir. A good portion will be in his own words. Although he wrote no books and few articles, I have had access to his charming and voluminous correspondence.

I have written in the hope that generations who never knew him may get some hint of his warmth and his spirit. Lewis Perry was in love with life. He knew his strengths and weaknesses, but he neither bragged nor worried about them. If I meet him in a future world, he will be likely to thank me for my effort in writing this book and then be reminded of a story.

I am indebted to many people for their support on this project. Large numbers of Exeter alumni, emeriti, and faculty members and their wives have helped. Dr. Perry's secretaries and nurses have shared their memories. James Otis has generously shared with me his delightful correspondence with Lewis Perry. The librarians at Phillips Exeter Academy, Phillips Academy, Andover, Lawrenceville School, Williams College, and Princeton University have outdone themselves.

Mr. and Mrs. William J. Cox (Emily Perry), Mr. and Mrs. Lewis Perry, Jr., and Dr. and Mrs. William Peltz (Dr. Perry's stepdaughter and her husband) have encouraged me and helped in countless ways.

Mr. and Mrs. William N. Bates, Henry W. Bragdon, Henry F. Bedford, Thomas H. LeDuc, and Victor L. Cahn have made very valuable suggestions.

And David McCord, Lewis Perry's friend and mine for over 50 years, has written a most gracious foreword.

Most of all I thank my wife, Katharyn, for her research, her typing, and her helpful criticism. She loved Dr. Perry as much as I did.

WILLIAM G. SALTONSTALL

CONTENTS

ILLUSTRATIONS

LEWIS PERRY OF EXETER

A GENTLE MEMOIR

SMALL-TOWN BOY
1877–1898

Lewis perry was a small-town boy, in his words a product of "the old swimmin' hole," who had the good fortune to grow up in a large, colorful family in a New England college town. They were descendants of Scotch-Irish clothmakers who had emigrated from Hampshire, England, just after the Great London Fire of 1666 and who had settled first in Watertown, Massachusetts, but moved to Worcester in the eighteenth century.

Lewis's grandfather, the Reverend Baxter Perry, was born in Worcester in 1792 and graduated from Harvard in 1817 and from Andover Theological Seminary in 1820. He settled in Lyme, New Hampshire, where he was Congregational minister until his death in 1830 from a ruptured blood vessel in the brain, which occurred while he was plowing. His son, Arthur Latham Perry, born six weeks after his father's death, was the father of Lewis.

For almost forty years a popular professor of political economy at Williams College, Arthur Perry was an abrasive, eloquent, prickly man, described 100 years later by his son Lewis as "Scotch-Irish with all the trimmings." His son Carroll's sketch, entitled "A Professor of Life," written in 1923, gives us a delightful picture of this strong man. And the final paragraph could be judged a description of Lewis as well:

> He loved truth and honor and fairness; but mostly he loved friendship and little children. He cared nothing for riches, and only a little for fame. Some measure of the last he gained, and he knew what to do with it. He forgot it. If we hold with Bronson Alcott that heaven is a place in which we shall be able to get a little conversation, it is certain where you will find my father. You will find him, directly he has gotten "the lay of the land," where the wit is the keenest, the humor most humane, the laughter the heartiest, and the hope for mankind the most sure.

Arthur Latham Perry was a licensed preacher but not a minister. For forty years he took a leading part in the college chapel services, waging eloquent battle against cigarettes and alcohol. Those who used them, he warned, "have pitched their tents toward Sodom." He loved and wrote local histories, including one of Williamstown, which was full of frank and outspoken commentary on his contemporaries and which led to his social ostracism. Republicans, including several Williams College trustees, had strong reservations about this colorful and effective advocate of free trade.

He married Mary Smedley, the girl next door, a lady of patience, whose light touch could often calm her controversial husband. Her warmth, her sense of humor, and her remarkable gift for mimicry provided a balance to his strictness and irascibility and were inherited by their youngest son, Lewis.

The Perrys reared a family of six children born between 1858 and 1877: Grace, the oldest, a teacher; Bliss, professor of English at Princeton and Harvard and editor of the *Atlantic Monthly*; Walter, a banker working in Hartford and New Haven; Arthur, raconteur and mimic supreme; Carroll, an Episcopal rector with a parish in Ipswich, Massachusetts; and Lewis, born on January 3, 1877, the youngest. Bliss was his father's favorite; Lewis, his mother's. The family was once compared to a clump of Berkshire maples—good for everything from housebuilding and choice furniture to violin timber and maple sugar.

The Perry home on Spring Street in Williamstown, an ample white three-decker with porch and rockers, still stands. Large and high-ceilinged, the entrance faces Grace Court, named for Lewis's sister. The front door is inside the glassed-in porch, and the whole effect is similar to Lewis Perry's later Exeter home at 1 Abbot Place. A large living room lies to the left of the front door. To the right is the former study of Professor Arthur Latham Perry, a small square room with a fireplace. The dark red wall covering over the mahogany dado and the desk cluttered with piles of books and papers look much as they must have when the professor was writing his sermons and lectures. Behind the study are the kitchen and dining room. It is a large house, but Mary Perry fortunately had the help of servants for housework and cooking. In the old days water had to be carried up from a spring at the foot of Spring Street—probably one of the chores performed by Lewis and his four brothers.

Called the Old Sod, the family home housed the family of eight as well as many a group of missionaries, alumni, young people, and assorted friends, through whom the children learned not only of the small New England town but of other parts of the country and the world outside. Presiding over all was Arthur Latham Perry, a man of resolute nature, hearty laugh, rugged speech, intense conviction, and indomitable purpose. Yet he demonstrated that such qualities need not be incompatible with love and gentleness.

Like his brothers, Lewis began his education at the school on Spring Street, run by the memorably strict principal Eli Herbert Botsford. From there the boys probably moved to one of several private junior high schools. All were fond of baseball, all used to hang around Tom MacMahon's livery stable (now the Chevrolet agency), and all enjoyed hikes and climbs. In many ways, surely, Lewis's childhood was unexceptional. Yet in 1935, looking back, Perry wrote to his old friend Dick Rice:

> We have both had very happy lives and I think about the happiest childhood of any boys I know. With Lawrence Saunders performing operations, and Nat Griffin writing about immortality, and you the great Byron authority of the world, and I snooping around the Infirmary at school, trying to cheer boys up, I think we all found our niche in the world.

No record exists of Lewis Perry's studies in the Spring Street school. A couple of notes, however, suggest his predilections at that time. One unsigned message, written in 1880, probably by Carroll, reads: "Ma, keep Lewis downstairs for the Lord's sake. I am studying hard and cannot stand it." A second, in the steeply sloping hand of nine-year-old Lewis, is to his brother Bliss, seventeen years his senior: "Carroll is progressing slowly in pitching. A ball ground has been made at the head of the street in the park, and we purchased a large number of bats and quite a fiew [*sic*] balls in Troy."

But if Lewis's devotion to formal education was something less than total, he was learning in other, perhaps equally lasting, ways. Surely he must have acquired a sense of public responsibility from the political talk heard at the dinner table three times a day, although Carroll and Walter seemed to have gathered much more from what their father said. And no doubt the steady parade of fascinating characters who sojourned in the house had their influence. One such figure was the "sawbuck" philosopher, Bill Pratt. Perry later described him:

A Williamstown character, a wood sawyer and stove blackener who had a most extraordinary vocabulary of words which he made up himself, meaningless in themselves, but when put into well-rounded sentences they had the appearance and the sound of something.

Here is a sample of Bill Pratt's remarkable prose:

This a funeral oration. Murmur and mourn.
The language of life is past. The grass of gullery
is gone and the electricity of the bay-rum tree is
decided with the laments of refuge. What a bur-
den he was! What a beautiful Pharisee! By the
corduroy of his attainments and the melody of
his magnificence he retired and the palms of his
pussy willows wave with the Rolling Ottaw.

Of his wife, Susan, Bill Pratt said, "She's got pi-
etude, she's got polidity, and all the ashialities of life."
As he came home at night, he would strike a forensic
attitude and proclaim, "Hail, diosity of the spheres!
Sanctify your mighty emblems!" No boy could listen without delight to such a jargon of wild, resonant, elementary nonsense, streaked with occasional
shrewdness and accentuated here and there by a curi-
ous yell of his own invention. And is it unfair to look
ahead to Perry's later love of drama and oratory and
trace at least some of its roots back to such a man?

Lewis also studied piano for a time, with limited
success, but the experience seems to have given rise to
a lifelong love of music. Decades later, in 1960, when
the new music building at Exeter was named for him,
Perry wondered what his old teacher Miss Rosalie
Smith would think:

I left her for an inferior teacher who gave me
buckwheat cakes and sausages with every lesson.
I learned but one piece called "Wild Rider" in
fast 2/4 time, but my father did not give up, because on Sundays I could play "Onward, Chris-

tian Soldiers" and "Now the Day Is Over"—my two *chef d'oeuvres*.

It was this same Rosalie Smith who wrote to him in 1945, chiding him about his contemplated retirement: "Here I be, pushin' eighty and 'gladly teaching' to beat the cars. What's more, I do my own housework. What are you planning to do in 1947? Eat griddle cakes, I suppose." A moved Perry replied, "It was lovely of you to write me as you did. I'm terribly sorry I didn't do better in my music, but I could not have more affection for you if I'd been a young Rubinstein." Lasting friendships were a Perry specialty.

Like most little boys, Lewis was afraid of the dark and used to dread delivering milk to the neighbors' back doors. Perhaps his acknowledgment of his own fear allowed him to become sympathetic to those with similar difficulties. More than once as an adult, he walked home hand in hand with a delivery boy, Ernest Gillespie, who later became acting principal of the academy, but who as a small boy felt safe and secure after dark in the understanding company of Dr. Perry.

In the fall of 1890 his father decided that Lewis, then thirteen years old, should attend Phillips Academy, Andover, from which brother Carroll had been graduated a few years before. Lewis's brief experience there was happy except for his difficulty with Latin. He was not well prepared for his class with Professor David Comstock ("Commie" to generations of Andover men) and wrote on October 6, 1890, to his sister, Grace:

I have been working hard ever since I came and I had to study two hours on my Latin and arithmetic and about an hour and a half on my English. I guess I will tell you what happened last week in Latin. Thursday I had my Latin well, but Friday "Commie" sent me to the board and told me to translate something and I got it wrong. He called me up after lesson and asked me what was the matter and was very kind to me. Saturday I worked hard on my lesson, but he caught me again. I made up my mind that I would know Monday's lesson, and studied it very hard but I seemed in a streak of horrible luck and last Wednesday I broke it. I hope I will never get in a place like that again.

After recounting some social occasions, Lewis closed with a P.S.: "Please do not say anything about the Latin."

Lewis's father was hardly so patient with Comstock and Andover. Lewis was grateful for "Commie's" friendship, but his father was outraged when Comstock suggested tutoring at extra expense. On October 22, 1890, he wrote a fiery letter to Dr. Cecil Bancroft, headmaster of Andover, which culminated:

I have had intimate and competent sources of information from another boy who was two years in his class and who was strongly (I may almost say desperately) opposed to my sending Lewis to Andover on account of the boorishness and Assinineness [*sic*] Combined prevalent in certain classrooms there. I have known for years from

other sources altogether that the *lack of common
decency* as towards pupils and patrons has
wrought more harm to Phillips Academy than
all other causes.

The letter concluded with the threatened withdrawal
of Lewis.

Years later, after his retirement as principal of
Exeter, Perry recounted the incident in a speech to
Andover alumni:

> Both Mr. Comstock and my father were
> Scotch-Irish and finally my father became so
> angry that he told me I couldn't go back to An-
> dover but that I could go to any preparatory
> school I chose. . . . I know that my father was
> wrong in the discussion. Mr. Comstock was the
> best friend I had at Andover, except Mr. Ban-
> croft, but I was young and had been brought up
> to mind my father, so with many regrets I left.

Yet his memory of Andover remained strong, he went
on, for "It was an honest place and a generous place
with high standards of scholarship."

Alfred Stearns, later to succeed Dr. Bancroft, was
four years ahead of Perry at Andover, and he, too, experienced "Commie" as Latin teacher. Stearns later
wrote to Perry that "if Comstock, from another world,
can still look down on what has happened in the world
he left behind him, I wonder what his reaction must
be as he sees two of the former pupils he maligned
enthroned as heads of the two famous Phillips Academies."

Lewis Perry stayed at home for the latter part of the fall of 1890. During his summers at Williamstown he had known some Lawrenceville School boys whom he liked, and so after Christmas he enrolled there. On the very first day of school, feeling lonely and a bit lost, he found himself speaking with a young man named Moreau Delano. The two immediately became chums and remained friends for life. Years later Delano recalled how Perry and a friend, as second formers at Lawrenceville, jointly purchased a book on etiquette for fifty cents, hoping to gain the favor and attention of some young lady who was much in vogue those days in school circles.

The Lawrenceville experience was interrupted, however, when Arthur Perry grew ill. Lewis, the only one in the family who could make his father laugh, went home to help his mother. He probably spent his eleventh-grade year at Williamstown High School, then returned to Lawrenceville for his senior year.

Lewis found Lawrenceville a friendly, happy, busy place. His academic record was good except in mathematics. He achieved honors in English literature, composition, and rhetoric, especially elocution, declamation, and oratory, but met with less success in algebra and geometry. He took virtually no science. In 1892, as a tenth grader, he recited "The Jackdaw of Rheims" by Richard Harris Barham, winning a second prize in declamation. He was a careful student of oratory throughout his life, much as his father had been. As a senior he was also associate director of the upper house with specific responsibilities in the Tennis Association.

Perhaps most important, Perry's lifelong interest in dramatics first bloomed at Lawrenceville, where he helped found the Dramatic Club. He commenced his acting career by playing Juno in *As You Like It, Up to Date*, which was staged in the old gym. The story concerns Juno, who has enchanted a certain rock so that any man who lies upon it falls in love with the first girl that passes. Naturally complications ensue, the type of shenanigans Perry enjoyed all his life.

His range of extracurricular activities at Lawrenceville was hardly limited, however. He played tennis and baseball, although his batting average of .142 suggested he would never become a masterful hitter. As a senior he was managing editor of *The Lawrence*, and his editorials urged more support for tennis, elocution, dramatics, and school cheering. But even at this stage of his life his oratorical skills were recognized. In March 1894 he was toastmaster at the twenty-eighth anniversary of the Philomathean Society, and in June he offered the class valedictory. Its concluding lines suggest values he stressed throughout the rest of his life:

> As the class of 1894 leaves, it is our hope that we have helped and not hindered this school's progress; we have shown class spirit, yet '94 can honestly say, "first the school and then the class."

Lawrenceville was much to Lewis's liking. Few New Englanders attended, but he found a gracious welcome and an amused acceptance of his manner of speech. He also met teachers who were both scholarly and tolerant, and the combination made a deep im-

pression on him. Among these was Charles Henry
Raymond, a mathematics teacher from New England.
Perry later recalled:

> One day after acute discouragement when I
> had failed to solve any of the five problems cor-
> rectly, I summoned enough courage to ask this
> man if when he was a boy he liked arithmetic.
> His answer was properly high-minded and aca-
> demic, but the affectionate, quizzical, and under-
> standing smile which he gave meant a lot, and I
> learned a valuable lesson—that it is possible for a
> boy to be a little stupid without being abnormal.

He remembered as well:

> . . . teachers who cared for books but who had
> little time to read them. I found, too, men who
> cared for music and art and were not ashamed to
> say so, and here of course I met intellectual giants
> in the upper forms.

Such experiences made telling impressions on the
young Perry. It is probably fair to say that he himself
was not an extraordinarily gifted man, although certainly he had abilities in dramatics and athletics. But
just as endemic to his character was an appreciation
of the value of such talent in others, as well as the
willingness to encourage its development. A teacher
can have no more important qualities, and Perry was
blessed with both.

He also emerged from Lawrenceville with a healthy
skepticism about judging people, especially young

people. One of his teachers told him that he was a little suspicious of what was then called the new psychology. Years later Perry remarked that in his experience "either mothers exaggerate to me what psychiatrists tell them about the abilities of their sons or else psychiatrists exaggerate to mothers, or else the science is still in its infancy." In any case, he learned to trust his own good judgment above all.

In the fall of 1894 Lewis Perry came to Williams College, from which his father had resigned his professorship three years before. Although Lewis probably lived at home in the Old Sod, he was involved in a wide range of college activities: studies, drama, athletics, and fraternity life.

As in secondary school, Perry was less than a brilliant scholar at Williams. He did good work in English, elocution, and history but, as always, had a hard time with mathematics and science. During most of his four years he studied languages (Greek, Latin, French, and German) but did not pursue them to the point of fluency. In January 1896 he wrote to Bliss about his courses: "This is the first time I can remember when I have felt on an equal footing with the rest of the class as far as the studies went, but I mean to get something this term and be in earnest about it."

His primary interest, as an undergraduate and later as a member of the faculty, was drama. Indeed, he made such an impression that fifty years later, on September 24, 1956, Senator Herbert H. Lehman wrote to him:

I remember with particular pleasure my association with you in *Cap and Bells*. I have never understood how I ever qualified even for very lowly parts in the plays we did. I have a feeling, however, that if you had continued your career as an actor, you would have been nearly as successful in that field as you were for so long as Headmaster of Exeter. You certainly showed great talent and I still chuckle over some of your comedy scenes.

Perry was in the Williams dramatic club for three years and president for one. Simultaneously he had charge of dramatics in Williamstown High School. In his senior year *Cap and Bells* toured through North Adams, Troy, Pittsfield, and Williamstown with a production of *The Rivals*, in which he played the part of Acres.

Perry was as well a good athlete in college. He never became a strong hitter in baseball, but he played a clean second base. Above all, he was an outstanding tennis player. As president of the Tennis Association he repeatedly won his matches in both doubles and singles against Amherst and Dartmouth.

Tennis became an eternal passion of his. He played in many tournaments between 1900 and 1914, to the point where his young wife, Margaret, bemoaned his frequent absence on the tennis circuit. One of the highlights of these years was the summer of 1901, when Perry and his partner won a sterling silver tankard, emblematic of second prize in the national doubles tournament of the United States National

Lawn Tennis Association. Although not a hard hitter, he played a control game, making superb use of the curving slice. Exeter students in the twenties frequently admired his skill on the court. As late as 1942 my wife teamed up with him for a doubles match against a faculty couple, and he continued to play the game until he was nearly seventy.

As with all aspects of Perry's life, tennis, too, had its moments of great humor. After his retirement from Exeter he was invited to speak at a Dartmouth alumni dinner in Boston, where he recalled playing in Hanover in 1896 against Dartmouth's best player. They were going at it intensely before a large audience when in the middle Perry had to run and stretch in order to retrieve a drop shot. In so doing, however, he popped two buttons in his fly. He tried to carry on but after three or four points realized the impossibility. He went to the net and asked his opponent, a member of a rival fraternity, if he could get a safety pin. After a fruitless search, the opponent beckoned to Perry and gave him his fraternity pin, an irreverence calculated to "psych out" any normal player. The Dartmouth alumni laughed so loudly over the story that the outcome of the match was never learned!

While Perry was a student at Williams, the college was never beaten in singles or doubles. "Those were the great days," he wrote in 1934:

In the spring of '98 Howard Doughty and I won the doubles at Amherst one Friday afternoon, then I won the singles, and the next morn-

ing I took my final examination in English in
the Amherst library, played in the baseball game
that afternoon, and gave in my examination paper in the seventh inning to Mr. Hancock, who
was Professor of English. That could not quite be
done in these days.

Perry was a popular, respected member of the Williams community, and he devoted himself enthusias-
tically to a variety of clubs and social activities. He
was president of the Williams Lawrenceville Club
and a member of both the Bohemian Club and the
Gargoyle Society. President of the Williams chapter
of Alpha Delta Phi, he later served as the fraternity's
national president. He was also president of the Class
of 1898 and a member of the Honor Committee. He
acted as toastmaster at his freshman banquet, and in
1898 he delivered the Address to the Lower Classes
entitled "Smoking the Pipe." In his class poll he was
voted "second most popular" and "second most fascinating." At the Senior Class Supper on June 23, 1898,
he spoke on the topic "Beyond the Gates." The gist
of his remarks: "The Lord knows what we may find,
dear lass, and the deuce knows what we may do." He
was also elected choragus of his class at Williams'
104th commencement. His interest in the community
was made clear by his presidency of the Boy Scout
Council and by his help in founding the Williamstown Boys' Club.

During two of his college summers Perry worked
for the New York City Recreation Department in a
park on Second Avenue, where hundreds of Irish and

Jewish children played. He visited many of their homes, and his eyes were opened to a side of life not found at Lawrenceville and Williamstown. Living in a room "under the Brooklyn Bridge, [he] slept in a hammock and was paid a salary of eight dollars per week." Yet he knew how valuable the experience was. As he later wrote, "[The work] did me more good than anything that had happened to me up to that time. Life had looked pretty rosy until I lived with those people down in the slummiest part of the slums for two summers." Surely such understanding and sympathy would serve him well in the years to come.

In the autumn of 1898, following his graduation from Williams, Perry went to Princeton to work for an M.A. in English literature. Bliss had been on the Princeton faculty since 1893, and he invited his much younger brother to stay with him during his year of study. While doing his graduate work, Lewis taught part time at Princeton Preparatory School.

In an interview with Henry Bragdon, Perry reflected upon his graduate education:

> To me Princeton was intellectually my birthplace. It was the most genial, happy place I have ever known. The circle of men with whom my brother was most friendly were almost to a man intellectually alive.

Certainly the highlight of the experience was a course with Woodrow Wilson, soon to be promoted to the presidency of the college and then elected President of the United States. Perry was fascinated by Wilson, thinking him "the greatest man I had ever seen, enormously stimulating." The Wilsons did not hold open houses for students in the evening, but Professor Wilson often engaged Perry and other students in conversation. More than once he asked Perry to sit with him on the train to New York. Bragdon reports that the two became so close as to play golf together.

Thirty or forty years ago I used to invite Principal Perry to conduct my American history classes when we were dealing with Woodrow Wilson. He never failed to bring to these classes his warm admiration of Wilson and his opinion that the country had let him down on the League of Nations issue because of his tragic overconfidence.

When Wilson became president of Princeton, he asked Perry to be his first preceptorial scholar. Looking back on this honor in March 1959, Perry recalled that he gave it up because of his father's illness, although he himself was eager to accept it. At the same time, despite the flattering offer, Perry never quite felt sure of himself as a scholar who could reach the highest echelons of a university. "I was, however," he consoled himself, years later, "pretty good as Principal of Exeter, even if I do say so myself."

In the spring of 1898 Perry wrote to James C. Mac-Kenzie, an Exeter graduate and headmaster of Lawrenceville, inquiring about a job teaching English and elocution. No opening was available that fall, but he won the job for the next year and so in 1899 entered his first year of full-time teaching.

Thus, the "bucolic boy from the country," as he called himself, had grown up. He had matured in

Victorian times, but he was not in most respects a Victorian. Certainly he had a social conscience and a natural sympathy for people which guided him all his days. And at the same time he enjoyed so much of his life: teaching, studying, acting, and playing tennis.

But in his own way Lewis Perry was committed to people. Though not a man of towering intellectual accomplishment, he valued such achievement in others. Indeed, he valued ability of all kinds and devoted his life to its development. Most of all, he emerged from his youth a man of uncommon graciousness and affability. People instinctively felt a kinship with him.

Now he was embarking upon a career for which he was superbly qualified and which would enable him to synthesize all the qualities that made him special.

FROM "GREAT MAN'S BOY TO GREAT BOYS' MAN"

1899–1914

❧ॐ❧

I<small>N THE</small> fall of 1899, with his Princeton M.A. in hand, Lewis Perry began two years of teaching at his old school, Lawrenceville. His part-time work at Princeton Preparatory School in 1898–1899, done while working for his degree, was not especially demanding. But Lawrenceville and its house plan placed heavy responsibilities on the young teacher of English and elocution. In addition to his academic duties, he served as associate master of Dickinson House as well as coach of dramatics, tennis, and baseball. In rare moments of relaxation he would walk to Princeton and back, a twelve-mile hike. "Those were the days before motors came along."

In a speech given at the 125th anniversary of the school, Perry looked back on his Lawrenceville years, emphasizing his own growth:

I learned that men were more important than methods. I learned that the essential quality of every good school is its teachers. I learned the importance of play in a school. I learned that a good school must be a place of understanding. What makes a school an understanding place comes from the waitresses and workmen on the grounds, as well as teachers and patrons.

He never forgot his debt to Lawrenceville, either as student or teacher.

In 1901, then twenty-four years old, Perry joined the faculty of Williams College as instructor in English and elocution. In 1904 he was promoted to assistant professor, and in 1911, after aggressively writing to President Harry Garfield, he was promoted to professor. Yet he had not been sure whether he should accept that original appointment, and in a letter to Bliss, then editor of the *Atlantic Monthly*, his own academic insecurities manifested themselves once more:

It strikes me as queer that I should come back to teach in town. I am going right over the life of my youth—Lawrenceville-Williams-Lawrenceville-Williams—and I feel exactly as I did before my freshman year. I shall try to improve on my former record. I have been in a kind of reflected light from you, ever since I left college. My confidence in my own ability to succeed is shaken a good deal. If I can stand on my own legs perhaps I'll pull through.

Many years later, in a speech to the Society of
New England, Perry recounted, in typically self-
deprecating manner, the story of his first lecture at
the college:

> My subject, I blush to say, was Elocution, and
> having exhausted all that was ever known about
> the subject in thirty minutes I attempted to use
> up the next thirty by giving in glittering array
> the names of the great orators of history. I began
> with Demosthenes, interpreted the oratorical
> powers of St. Paul, and ended by showing how a
> late Secretary of State got his effects. And still
> the bell did not strike.

Having exhausted the material for the whole semester,
Perry fell back on the time-honored device of beginning teachers and asked, "Are there any questions?"

A hand shot up in the back row. "Is there any way
of getting out of this course?"

A later teacher at Williams, William Taeusch, had
a similar experience. "I often wonder," he says,
"whether Lewis told me this tale as anticipatory sol-
ace, but I have blessed him for fifty-seven years for
alleviating my despair."

But all reports indicate that the young instructor
invigorated freshman work in English and in particular aroused undergraduate interest in dramatics
and literature. He taught a course in composition to
freshman, corrected junior and senior themes, and,
in spite of his difficult first lecture, conducted an effective class in elocution. In 1908 he completed an edition

of Marlowe's *The Jew of Malta*. And he offered one of the first courses in American literature. Later he taught a variety of subjects: Elizabethan drama, prose writers of the nineteenth century, American colonial writers, and English drama from 1642 to the present. His handwritten notebooks of 1902–1903 show the care and thoroughness with which he prepared his classes. Selected portions of Chaucer and Spenser were assigned to be memorized. Perry loved as well the Elizabethans and the Romantic Movement and took long notes on readings from Milton, Byron, Keats, Shelley, Coleridge, Wordsworth, Browning, and Tennyson. He was also much attracted to the ancients like Plato, Pindar, and Sappho.

Perry's great success with students resulted, as it always would, more from personal charisma, genuine friendliness, and trained dramatic ability than from scholarship. His intense love of the theater, which he knew so well and was fond of discussing for hours on end, had much to do with his success as a teacher and later on as a principal. And his poise on the platform, knowledge of the elocutionist's art, and sense of the dramatic certainly help explain his later success as a public figure.

Much as Professor Perry loved teaching, he found time to be an active member of Alpha Delta Phi. His father had been in this fraternity but later thought fraternities did more harm than good and directed his sons not to join. But by the time he retired Arthur Perry had relaxed his rule "so that Lewis, who had already been excused from learning how to milk (the only real blot on his career in the opinion of his older brothers), was allowed the additional indulgence of joining a fraternity."

After a time Professor Perry began to reach beyond New England for his experience. In 1906 he went abroad with Bliss and met his old friend Billy James, portrait painter and son of the philosopher William James. The three walked and climbed and made friends in England, France, Belgium, Switzerland, and Italy. It was Billy James who offered a remark that would become one of Perry's maxims: "It does not matter so much what we accomplish as what we are in our daily lives."

The young college professor also extended himself intellectually. He studied English literature on a leave of absence at the Sorbonne, and he taught at New York University in the summer of 1911, staying at the Alpha Delta Phi Club on Forty-fourth Street. His reputation spread beyond the world of Williams as well. He was offered an opportunity to join the faculty at the University of Minnesota and in December 1912 was offered and declined the presidency of Wells College in Aurora, New York, "at a salary of $5,000 and the free occupancy of a house."

But as things would turn out, his most significant encounter occurred at the home of his classmate James Pratt, professor of philosophy at Williams. There Professor Perry met S. Sidney Smith, president of the Exeter trustees. No record of their conversation exists, but it is likely that Perry first learned of Exeter's interest in him about this time. He and Smith shared a very high regard for Dr. Amen, Exeter's principal.

And three years later, when a search committee was seeking a successor to Dr. Amen, Smith strongly supported the recommendation of Perry by William de-Witt Hyde, president of Bowdoin College.

During his years at Williams Professor Perry had been courting Margaret Hubbell, whose family were summer residents of Williamstown. The couple became engaged and were married on November 12, 1911. Reluctantly she allowed him to continue his out-of-town speeches and seemingly endless series of tennis matches, but she was unhappy over every absence. She wrote him frequently, addressing him as "Huck Finn" and "Lupin," signing her warm, affectionate letters "from the little grey house" and "Miss Margery."

In February 1914, during his last year as a member of the Williams faculty, Professor Perry was the speaker at the Williams Alumni Dinner in New York. In a revealing speech, Perry regaled his audience, one alumnus reported, "with a disquisition delightfully conceived and effectively delivered, on some of the characters of the campus and town." He spoke of the missionary tradition of Williams and described the college in its relation to the community. And he returned once again to Bill Pratt, the sawbuck philosopher, to quote a few of his memorable creations. At the heart of the speech was this thought: "Give me the wisdom of an honest but unaffiliated citizen of some deep-rutted college village lying in the hills."

Such a sentiment was properly reflective of Perry, and to understand it is to understand a good part of the man. Though in many ways his tastes and man-

ners were aristocratic, he nonetheless retained an
ability to befriend people of all social strata. He was
a man who disliked fronts or superficialities which
prevented the natural flow of feeling and thought,
and as a consequence, he had a remarkably wide range
of acquaintanceships. Consider this report from *The
Rectory Family*, by John Franklin Carter:

> In those days the town not only tolerated but
> was proud of an old woman named Mandy Crum
> who lived by herself, wore men's clothing,
> smoked a pipe, never washed, and whose cabin
> was full of innumerable cats. Where she got her
> money for tobacco was a profound mystery, but
> she remained in her filthy little shack, engaged
> in lively repartee with anyone who chose to dis-
> turb her. Lewis Perry was such a favorite of hers
> that she observed that of all the roosters in her
> flock, she had named the one that crowed the
> loudest, Lewis.

Perry would offer that same generosity of spirit to
generations of Exeter students.

During these years in Williamstown, Professor
Perry made notes on what he called the teacher's philosophy. These were excerpts from the writings of men
like William deWitt Hyde, Charles W. Eliot, George
Herbert Palmer, and William Lyon Phelps, but they
throw light on his own beliefs about teaching. Here
are a few examples:

> One cannot teach at all who does not know
> his subject; one cannot teach well who does

not know his students; one cannot know his students who has not previously known intimately and appreciatively scores of other persons, either in literature or in life, or preferably both.

Is my interest in my work so contagious that my pupils catch from me an eager interest in what we are doing together?

Do I get at the individuality of my students so that each one is different to me from every other, and I am something no other person is to them?

The four essentials to success as a teacher—a teacher must have an aptitude for vicariousness; an already accumulated wealth; an ability to invigorate life through knowledge; a readiness to be forgotten.

The capacity of the human mind to resist the introduction of knowledge cannot be overestimated.

I love to teach. I love to teach as a painter loves to paint, as a musician loves to play, as a singer loves to sing, as a strong man rejoices to run a race.

Teaching is a cause to be served, not a job to be done.

Personal influence is not an affair of acting but of being.

In his years on the Williams faculty, Professor Perry earned respect as a stimulating teacher and a delightful gentleman, full of stories about his colleagues and students. Most significantly, he no longer felt he was "Bliss's little brother." In fact, on one occasion, Bliss returned to Williamstown from Cambridge and wished to use the college library. He found it closed but beckoned to a janitor inside. The janitor opened the door and asked him what he wanted.

"I'd like to take out a book."
"Who are you?"
"I'm Professor Perry."
"You are not! Professor Perry is a good friend of mine. What is your first name?"
"Bliss."
"There ain't no such first name. Come back later after the library is open."

With such renown supporting him, Professor Perry was able to take in stride Bliss's later joking comment "Lewis, for a man with your limitations you have gone a long way!" And his spirits were buttressed by one appreciative student who wrote to him in a tone which would be reheard so often in years to come:

You taught me a great many things in my formative years. While a lot of them had to do with poetry and drama and matters of that sort, there were other facets such as integrity, fairness, humor, and the joy of living. For better or for worse, you cannot escape some responsibility for what I have become. I hope to be a credit to your teaching, as you have been a credit to the cause of education.

Before he went to Williams, Perry had had a diffidence about him, a tentativeness. Perhaps it stemmed from his being the youngest in a family of considerable accomplishment. Whatever the cause, he had to *grow* into "a great boys' man." And possibly it was this struggle that he himself underwent that made him so tolerant and responsive to the struggles of his students.

In any case, it was an assured Lewis Perry who in June 1914, just as his life seemed so settled and secure, received word that the Phillips Exeter Academy trustees wished him to become principal of the academy.

Many years later, as he looked back, his words reflected that new confidence; "Teaching was going well, I thought. I had elective courses, and only those who wanted to have me were in the courses, but for once I chose the harder thing and went to Exeter."

PERRY JOINS THE "GIANTS"
1914–1929

❧

PHILLIPS EXETER ACADEMY was 133 years old when Lewis Perry became its eighth principal. The man he succeeded, Dr. Harlan P. Amen, had served from 1895 to 1913.

Amen gave the academy direction. When he took over, the moral and intellectual standards were lax, and the respect between students and faculty was nonexistent. Amen held to fair standards, which became the basis for strict and just discipline. He did not hesitate to expel deadwood, among either faculty or students. And above all, Amen instilled in all members of the school community a confidence in themselves and the institution. An indefatigable worker, Amen left to his successor a school among the best in secondary education in America.

On November 7, 1913, Amen conducted chapel and spoke to the school about the next day's football game with Andover. But he did not live to see the 59–0 Exeter triumph which ended seven years of defeats.

On Saturday morning he suffered a stroke, never re-
gained consciousness, and died on Sunday afternoon.

A search committee of three trustees was established to find a new principal: Jeremiah Smith, Jr.,
Robert Winsor, and William deWitt Hyde. Hyde,
president of Bowdoin College, had been Amen's room-
mate at Exeter and had strongly urged Amen's selection as principal. Now, along with Jeremiah Smith,
Jr., he took a leading part in bringing Perry to the
academy. Recently Hyde had solicited advice from
Professor Perry about a key appointment in Bowdoin's
English Department. So helpful was Perry's response
that Hyde remembered him when the Exeter position
became vacant.

On May 5, 1914, Perry received a long letter from
his brother Carroll, an Episcopal minister in Ipswich,
Massachusetts, urging him to accept the position if
offered it. A graduate of Andover, Carroll had heard,
along the grapevine, rumors of Lewis's impending
appointment. After describing the principal's residence and how Lewis would be able "almost at once,
on the excellent salary, to fix up the house in suitable
fashion," Carroll concluded:

This is a great chance to do a big piece of work
and to make a place for yourself second to none
in this particular line. You have more personality
and drawing power than either Stearns [An-
dover] or Sam Drury [St. Paul's] and just see
what success they are achieving. Don't hesitate
to take this offer! It is a real *call*, and you have
the powers. I am proud of you and your success

thus far, but many would say that *this* is your preordained task and there are few who can stand up to it as you can.

On June 18, 1914, Lewis and Margaret lunched with President Hyde and some trustees. Since both candidate and trustees were ardent baseball fans, it seemed natural for them to take in a Red Sox game before retiring to Boston's Union Club for final discussion and vote on the position.

The committee on filling the existing vacancy in the office of Principal reported and after discussion it was unanimously voted that Lewis Perry of Williamstown, Massachusetts, Professor of English Literature in Williams College, be elected Principal of the Phillips Exeter Academy.

The salary offered was $6,000 a year plus a home. Stearns, brother Bliss, and Perry's old friend Moreau Delano all urged him to accept the job. On June 20, 1914, he sent a telegram to the trustees: "Accept position with deep sense of honor and responsibility." He had never been to the town of Exeter nor had he seen the academy. But he later wrote Bliss, "Exeter has never been very far from Williamstown." True, the towns were indeed similar, but the step from professor to principal was a big one.

The office to be filled, as Perry would always insist, was that of principal instructor, not headmaster. The academy's original deed of gift from its founder, John Phillips, provided in 1781 that the principal should be "of good natural abilities and literary acquirements, of a natural aptitude for instruction and government. A good acquaintance with human nature is much to be desired." The title has been usually shortened to "Principal," but like most of his predecessors and successors, Perry hoped to instruct not only as chief executive officer from the assembly platform but as classroom teacher of English and coach of dramatics. His old friend Frank Sayre reminded him that "it's a good thing to have a job that's beyond your capacity." Perry was to have the challenge he wanted.

He received many letters congratulating him on his appointment. In answer to a long letter of good advice from Dr. Samuel Drury, rector of St. Paul's School, Perry answered with characteristic modesty:

> I feel that I shall need at least two years to get hold of the situation there and get hold of my own job. I shall need advice and encouragement and I shall certainly avail myself of your kind offers in those directions. It is all strange to me and I am a perfect stranger to Exeter, but I shall do my very best to uphold the traditions of the school and to give a progressive administration at the same time. That is not the easiest thing in the world to do, but I want to make it my life work.

In 1914 the town of Exeter was a quiet head of tidewater. Coasting schooners picked up and delivered their cargoes to other East Coast ports. A cotton mill and brickyard were thriving. The first automobiles were scaring horses on the dirt roads, while trolley lines connected with neighboring towns. Boston was about two hours to the south on the Boston and Maine Railroad.

Weeks and Seward at the old Merrill Drug Store beckoned, "Try our hot chocolate fudge on ice cream." The Rexall Store claimed, "Queen Bess and Fluffy Ruffles our specialty," and the Academy Grill dispensed its time-honored "peanut betweens" and "hickey and heavies." Silent movies were shown in the Exeter Opera House, and Mrs. Roberta Richmond continued her dancing lessons at 14 Pine Street, giving instruction in the hesitation, lame duck, the half-and-half, waltzes, tango, and one-step as well as the new ballroom creations: Lulu fado, gavotte, fox-trot, and Castle polka.

Typical of the town's reaction to the new principal was that of one of the members of the school's grounds crew, John McNulty. In August 1914 he was suffering from a painful malady and was told by his doctor to enter the hospital immediately for an operation. "No," said John, "I'll go to the hospital after I get this new man moved into the principal's house."

The academy was close to the center of the town, and its 569 boys were taught by a faculty of 30 men. Many of the students were lodged in the homes of townspeople, where they could exercise more independence than could their counterparts in most other schools.

Perry later recalled the first day he saw Exeter:

It was in July 1914, and the hottest and moistest day I can remember. I had come up to the town by train with Mr. S. Sidney Smith who was

the President of the Trustees. He insisted on wait-
ing at the station until Dunk Lord, the driver of
the hack, put down the top, so in state we drove
up Lincoln Street and through the playing fields.
The thing that impressed me most on that drive
was a lovely stretch of the Squamscott River right
below Harriet Tilton's house.

The occasion of that first visit, however, was hardly
a casual one. On July 3, 1914, two weeks after Perry's
election as principal, the academy's main classroom
building was destroyed by fire. Perry received word
while visiting friends on Naushon Island. The trustees
met on July 6 at the Union Club in Boston and re-
quested that the architects Cram and Ferguson make
sketches for a new building. At a meeting on July 15,
held at Beacon Street, with the new principal present,
they appointed a building committee composed of
Perry, Jeremiah Smith, and S. Sidney Smith. By July
29 the school had learned that the insurance on the
old building would amount to $56,750 but that the
new structure was to cost four times that amount. Yet
on October 9 the new building was dedicated. On November 5 the cornerstone was laid. And on December
15 all the funds necessary had been promised. The
remarkably swift progress was both a credit to the new
principal and a tribute to the school's faith in him.

On the morning of September 16, 1914, Perry was
formally introduced to the students at an assembly in
Phillips Church. The Reverend Samuel H. Dana conducted the devotions at which townspeople and visitors were present with students and faculty. When all

were seated, Dr. Dana said, "Boys, stand up." The
school rose. "This is your new principal, Dr. Lewis
Perry. Boys, sit down." In later years, Perry said, "I
have learned that the length of stay is in inverse ratio
to the grandeur of the ceremony." After the introduction and prolonged applause, Perry spoke, and one
section of his talk became famous:

> I am sure that the new boys this morning are
> anxious to know about the rules of the school.
> Someone has said about the rules of Exeter that
> there are no rules until they are broken. As long
> as a boy respects the freedom of this place, gets
> his lessons, and behaves himself as a gentleman
> should, he need not worry much about rules.

On September 16, 1914, *The Exonian*, the student
newspaper, welcomed the new principal on behalf of
the students:

> Since Professor Perry can combine a love of
> boys, a sense of humor, skill in athletics, a win-
> ning personality, and progressive educational
> ideas, Exeter seems truly fortunate to secure such
> a man. *The Exonian* extends a very hearty wel-
> come to our new Principal.

Finally, at the New England Alumni Dinner on
December 14, Perry outlined what would be his credo
for more than thirty years to come:

> I believe in the Phillips Exeter Academy, her
> history, her traditions, her alumni. I believe in a
> classical education, an old-fashioned education. I

believe in athletics, the kind that means clean,
hard playing that never sacrifices the greater
glory of the game to the baser glory of winning
the prize. A school teacher who is not a born
teacher should never teach. One cannot be taught
how to teach. It is a gift that cannot be manu-
factured.

A brief note to Sidney Smith, written in the fall of
1914 after Exeter's football team had beaten Andover's, reaffirms such values:

We had a great victory on Saturday and a
magnificent celebration Saturday night. I was
even prouder of the school than I was of the team.
We have now turned from interest in athletics
and are living "the higher life" exclusively.

The academy was governed by a board of trustees,
some of whom were townspeople, and by the principal, but most of all by the faculty, which jealously
exercised considerable independent power. Winning
their solid backing was Perry's major accomplishment in 1914–1915, as it would be again from 1931
to 1933 when a large influx of younger men again
tested, then trusted, his leadership.

Perry found Exeter a more democratic place than
Williams, as was manifest in the spirit of such a
faculty member as Joseph S. Ford, assistant to the
principal and director of admissions. In Perry's words:

We had a pretty hard time that first year, but
I had so much work to do that I didn't mind. Joey
Ford was wonderful that summer, gettings things

into running order for the opening of school. He
was Assistant to the Principal and might have expected to be Principal, but he turned right
around, pitched in, and was loyal beyond words.

So were others like William A. Francis, Wentworth
Professor of Mathematics since 1887; George B. Rogers,
director of studies; James A. Tufts, secretary to the
faculty; John C. Kirtland, Morison Professor of Latin;
Arthur G. Leacock, Cilley Professor of Greek; and
Frank W. Cushwa, Odlin Professor of English. Con-
ceivably these men could have resented Perry as an
interloper, younger and in many ways less experienced in the life of a secondary school. But without a
trace of jealousy they rallied to the support of the
thirty-seven-year-old principal.

Equally important, Perry quickly gained the
friendship and support of leading townspeople like
John Templeton, editor of the *Exeter Newsletter*; Dan
Gilman, farmer; John Adams, railway agent; and
Judge Henry Shute. Shute, author, lawyer, and moving spirit in the town brass band, was an especially
solid supporter of Perry, as was Ned Shute, who was
considered the ne'er-do-well and black sheep of the
family.

But as Perry steadily gained the trust and respect
of the adult members of the community, so did he
quickly develop bonds with the boys, especially those
who found themselves in difficulties. John Cowles, '17,
of Des Moines, Iowa, a new student in the fall of 1914,
was desperately homesick. When Perry heard that he
was planning to withdraw, he immediately asked

young Cowles to dinner. Talking to the lonely boy, he said:

> I have just been made Principal. Although I have already discovered that this job is going to be much more difficult than I expected, you are my first specific problem. If you leave the school now, that will mean that I have failed on my first job here.

Cowles replied that he still expected to withdraw the next day, but when the principal suggested he come to dinner again with him and Mrs. Perry, he found the food and the company irresistible. Both Perry and Cowles hung on during their first year and became fast friends. Cowles stayed, was graduated, and became a valued trustee of the academy and publisher of the *Minneapolis Star-Tribune*.

Another early student whose life was brightened by the new principal was James F. Oates, Jr., '17, of Chicago. In 1916 Oates was failing almost all his courses, but he had been selected to play the title role in *Sherlock Holmes*.

> This was a big thrill and the most satisfying achievement in my life to date. *The Exonian* had a banner headline, "Oates chosen to be Sherlock." Everything was magnificent until later in the morning Dr. Clark, the Latin professor, said to me, "Oates, I want to see you after class." After class he said, "Oates, you cannot be in that play; your Latin is not good enough."
>
> I was heartbroken. I went in to James P. Web-

ber, the English teacher in charge of the play, and with tears in my eyes said I couldn't be in the play. Dr. Webber sorrowfully said, "Well, there is nothing I can do for you. The only man that can help is the Principal."

I made an engagement to see Dr. Perry at his home in the later afternoon. I can hear the crunching snow as I walked across the yard. Dr. Perry sat down in front of the fire and said, "What can I do for you, Jim?" I told him that Dr. Clark said I couldn't be in the play. After a little talk Dr. Perry said that when he went to college, whenever there was a play, he was in it, and he always did his best work in the month the play was produced. "And since I think that you are just like me, you can be in the play."

This was a turning point in my life. I was given a chance, and I made good use of it. Pop Clark played his part and gave me the highest mark that I had had in the entire year in the month the play was produced.

No wonder Jim Oates later looked forward to Perry's annual visits to Chicago!

Such unilateral action may seem surprising but it reflects two aspects of Perry as principal. One was his confidence to do what he believed to be right, to stand up for his own educational principles. The other was his accessibility to students, a willingness to meet with them and to work sympathetically to solve their problems for their own benefit and for the good of the school.

He was not always the rugged individualist, however. During the early years of his principalship, he kept close counsel with Al Stearns of Andover. In particular, the two compared notes on candidates for admission, tallying acceptances and rejections and analyzing candidates' athletic ability, College Board results, and military training. Typical of their correspondence was Perry's request of Stearns:

> Will you tell me confidentially what you know about this boy? He doesn't seem to be, from what I have heard, one of the finest forms of our 20th century civilization. It is quite remarkable what news you get from little birds in this business.

But more serious issues were arising. As the United States entered World War I, both schools faced brand-new challenges, and Perry wrote to Stearns to affirm that they could weather the difficulties more effectively by sharing them:

> No schools should be more mutually dependent on each other than ours, and any success which comes to one is really shared by both. I feel that our chance as Principals to help the cause of education is great!

Yet Perry and Stearns had somewhat different attitudes toward the conduct of interscholastic athletics during the war. On April 17, 1917, after Stearns had canceled a series of contests, Perry wrote:

> While we cannot live lives which are quite normal at such a time as this, I feel the more the

boys exercise and the more they get out of doors in good, legitimate sport, the better condition they will be in to render service. I feel that in a school like this the boys should be urged to finish out their work. It seems to me that athletic sports aid very materially in keeping down what might be called unnecessary excitement and uneasiness.

Yet the two shared as well an easy, bantering relationship. Perry frequently chided Stearns for being too busy, as he wrote in 1920:

The chief criticism I have of Andover and you is the fact that you are so blamed busy that we never seem to be able to sit down and have a talk. I don't have anything to do in the course of a year except sit around and smoke, and I don't see what you have to do.

Perry modestly refrained from describing his own working day, which began in chapel at seven forty-five each morning. He would spend from eight to one in his office, take a nap, then a walk across the playing fields from two to four, and finish up from four to six back in the office.

Although Perry's new duties no longer permitted tournament tennis, he remained in practice, playing often with students and members of the faculty. But tennis was not Perry's only athletic interest. Both he and Stearns were baseball enthusiasts and exchanged scouting reports on their best prospects. One April Perry wrote, "We have a shortstop named O'Toole. I do not know whether he is good or not, but his name has the right ring to it."

Such activities, however, were only temporary respite from Perry's major concern in 1917 and 1918: World War I and how the school should respond to it. He urged Exeter boys to continue their education, although many were eager to join the Ambulance Service or the "mosquito fleet" for coastal patrol. In response, the Exeter Military Training Club was formed to hold outdoor drills in fall and spring, repairing to the Town Hall in winter. Two hundred students were divided into three companies, and the battalion drilled four times a week. Rifles and uniforms were secured, and faculty members Percy Chadwick, Norman McKendrick, and Harry Sweet took charge, with the assistance of P. J. Kelly, '14, a student at West Point. Simultaneously the draft caused a sudden decrease in applications for admission, but thanks to the increasing reputation of the new principal and the skill of Mr. Ford, the school suffered no serious shrinkage in enrollment.

An occurrence that left Perry agonizingly helpless occurred during the autumn of 1918, when the school, still without an infirmary, experienced a severe epidemic of Spanish influenza. Seventy students became seriously ill. One died. The dismayed principal called it "an insidious, dastardly, cruel disease which doesn't play the game according to the rules," and he suffered what he later described as a nervous breakdown from the worries and pressures.

By 1920 Perry had come to know many of his fel-

low school heads, and he was accepted as a member
of their group. These "giants," like Stearns, Boyden,
Peabody, Sill, Taft of Taft School, St. John of Choate,
Winsor of Middlesex and Gummere of Penn Charter
were so used to dominating their own institutions
that they tended to become a bit parochial. Nevertheless, they appreciated the cosmopolitanism and
obvious skill of the new man at Exeter.

Yet Perry was different, in style and tone. The other
headmasters tended to be all-powerful within their
own institutions, and their faculties had comparatively little influence. Perry, however, shared his
power with his faculty, further encouraging them by
letting their ideas come to fruition. Above all, he
prized good teaching, and to inspire that, he even invited Harvard faculty members like Professor Albert
Bushnell Hart and Dean LeBaron Briggs to visit
classes and evaluate instruction at Exeter.

One who knew all the "giants," Sidney Lovett, former chaplain of Yale, commented:

> If I had to select one of the Chosen Six [school
> heads] with whom to share an existence, it would
> be Lewis Perry. He had all the basic virtues of
> the other five, plus an urbane sense of humor that
> was proof against boredom.

The many challenges of his new job obviously gave
Perry enjoyment. But the beauty and warmth in his
life were brought by Margaret and their infant son,
Lewis, Jr. Margaret worked as hard as her husband,
memorizing names of students, entertaining members

of the faculty and alumni, and getting to know people in town. It was a magnificent team effort.

Yet she still found it difficult to put up with his frequent absences, now devoted to school business rather than to tennis, and occasionally she released her frustrations. One day three of Dr. Perry's nicer traveling bags were in the downstairs hall, and as a friend calling upstairs on Mrs. Perry left, Margaret shouted, "Please give those bags a swift kick on your way out." But her concern for him never flagged. How often as he left the house was she heard to call out, "Have you got your rubbers on?"

The couple could always be counted on in an emergency. When the infant son of a faculty member died of burns, the Perrys immediately asked the parents to stay in the principal's house while they recovered from the worst of their hurt. It was an act of compassion, both typical and natural. In many ways the members of the faculty became an extension of the Perry family.

The new principal's early years were devoted primarily to achieving a solid financial base for the academy, and alumni support came quickly and generously. A capital drive for $2 million was completed in 1919. William Boyce Thompson, '90, a copper miner from Alder Gulch, Nevada, donated the new gymnasium and swimming pool. With Perry's help, the class of 1920 established Exeter's first annual giving appeal, the Christmas Fund, a small but steadily growing source of support for faculty salaries, scholarships, and the Principal's Discretionary Fund.

Perry, the master fund raiser, often raised money not by directly asking for it but by retelling a story, like the one about the collection box being passed at Sunday school in Williamstown. The teacher asked the students what the Bible says about giving. The first two little girls came through handsomely: "It is more blessed to give than to receive," and "Blessed are they that give to the poor." Then the teacher turned to a grubby little boy, who, as he dropped his pennies into the box, remarked, "A fool and his money are soon parted."

In 1920 a man who was to do much in shaping the academy's future, Edward S. Harkness, gave his first major gift to the school: $300,000 toward the endowment of teachers' salaries. Harkness and Perry had been friends ever since their chance meeting in 1902 on a night train as they both were headed toward a wedding in St. Paul, Minnesota. Both the young professor and the oil magnate were interested in education and the theater, and these common interests culminated in 1930 with a breathtaking contribution to the academy of $6 million. For the moment, however, Harkness's donation enabled Perry to raise faculty salaries, which then ranged from but $1,200 to $3,300 a year.

Typical of the financial problems Perry faced was a difficult tax case between the academy and the town, with the school paying its taxes each year under protest. The question was whether the dormitories could legally be taxed. Buildings used for instruction were tax-free, and although classes were not held in the dormitories, much individual instruction of a counseling nature did take place in them. Students learned as much in a well-run dormitory as in the classroom. Not until 1947 (a year after Perry retired) was the tax case finally settled by a compromise between the trustees of the academy and the selectmen of the town.

Once the solid financial base was established, Perry could turn toward developing the character of the academy. He accepted Exeter's strict training and tolerated no coddling, and he cared deeply about religion in the school. Daily chapel early in the morning, regular Sunday morning services, voluntary vespers and Bible classes, and the many service activities of the Christian Fraternity provided students with opportunities for an inquiring religious life. In 1919 the members of the Second Parish (Congregational) began renting Phillips Church for $1,000 a year. It was later sold to the school and is still in daily use.

In these years Perry began talking of Exeter as a "national school." In the academy's early days it drew its faculty and students largely from New Hampshire and the rest of New England, but during the Perry years it gradually attracted students from almost every state in the Union and from many foreign countries.

Perry's vision was beginning to take shape.

YEARS OF GROWTH
AND CHANGE
1921–1933

❧§❧

EXETER STUDENTS in the 1920s, including this writer, always agreed that the academy tested their mettle. For many it was a severe jolt, which awakened them for life.

Before the twenties Exeter boys had, for the most part, lived in the homes of townspeople. Gradually, at Perry's urging, the students began moving into accommodations on campus. While most teachers and students thought this innovation for the better, some were doubtful about herding boys into dormitories rather than letting them live in private rooming houses. True, the old arrangements linked academy and town in an important way, but consistent control was difficult. For instance, the rule that all lower classmen should be in their houses by 8:00 P.M. was hardly enforced uniformly.

Throughout this era Perry was surely the dominant presence in the students' lives. One graduate recalls that in 1922 Perry overruled a recommendation of the

Executive Committee, which had accused a boy of lying. Perry stated simply, "I know this boy. He could never speak an untruth." Perry cared enough to take the dangerous course of reversing the decision of an important faculty committee, taking a calculated risk that could have led to trouble had the faculty bridled.

Nor did he hesitate to influence the admissions process. One alumnus asked him why Exeter had accepted him and his three brothers, hardly renowned as scholars. Perry's answer was direct as always: "Your father had the boys, and Exeter needed the money." The applicant pool was not always as rich as it is now.

Perry continually encountered students under a variety of intriguing circumstances. In December 1920, for instance, one boy invited the future movie star Constance Bennett to the Exeter Prom, and with the rest of the guests she visited the Perrys for Sunday luncheon. Needless to say, she was the hit of the stag line, but the Perrys remained unflappable throughout the day.

In the winter of 1922 Mr. and Mrs. Thomas W. Lamont fulfilled an important need when they gave the school a modern infirmary. The Perry daily visits to the infirmary, often with goodies from the previous evening's dinner party, were good medicine for sick boys and encouraging to Miss Noyes and her colleagues on the small nursing staff.

The infirmary turned out to be a godsend in 1926, when a scarlet fever epidemic took its toll of the school. Webster Hall, a dormitory, had to serve as an infirmary annex as the top floor was given to the care of those who suffered unpleasant reactions to the inoc-

ulations given to the entire school. More than 200
boys became sick. Several suffered mastoid infections,
and one died. For a time it seemed as though the
school might have to be closed down. As he had been
in the influenza epidemic, Perry was worn out by
spring and again suffered what he later referred to as
a nervous breakdown.

Not long after, a doctor told him that it would help
prevent mastoids if boys were required to wear hats
in the winter. Therefore, from 1926 to 1946 Perry
imposed the rule that all students should wear hats
when out of doors in the winter term. A boy found
hatless was always given a severe warning, but the
definition of what qualified as a hat grew steadily
wider and vaguer!

Not all of Perry's decisions were public. He once
gave a senior a pass to go home to welcome his father's
return from prison. For four years Perry had kept the
senior's story a secret from students and faculty. That
was the manner of the man.

Precisely how was Perry regarded in the school
community? Surely the faculty was in support of him,
for otherwise he could not have taken the chances he
did by occasionally overriding their recommendations.
Still, a few veteran faculty members, such as James
Arthur Tufts, appointed in 1878, thought Perry as yet
young and inexperienced. But the principal never lost
patience with this fervent supporter of "the good old
days." "Tuffy" was my kindly faculty adviser in 1923,
and I recall that he regarded Perry as a boy still learning the ropes, who looked forward too much and back
too little.

What was the students' estimation? Most of us looked up to him as godlike but, like a Greek god, still quite capable of weakness and mistakes. We knew his humor; we knew his dramatic sense; we even knew his anger. There was steel in those velvet gloves. I remember one morning, just as chapel was about to begin. Among the stragglers making their way to their seats was a tall upper middler whose head had been close-shaved by some pranksters in his dormitory. Virtually the whole student body was anticipating his arrival. But when the rays of the sun bounced off that bald pate, Dr. Perry was furious. He stopped the boy in his tracks and ordered him to leave the room immediately and not to come back until properly hirsute. The boy did not return for several weeks.

Thus, our image of him was a formidable presence, not always intimately involved with students' lives, but a positive and good-natured force at the head of a school which was a powerful influence on so many of us during our most impressionable, character-building years.

To be sure, not all students were happy with the ways of Perry's Exeter. One alumnus recently described Exeter as "*a hateful place.* Looking back I wonder how I survived the exquisite knowing torture inflicted by older contemporaries." He commented on the abundance of men eighteen to twenty years old, dominating both athletic teams and dormitory life. At the same time this graduate was grateful for the academic discipline imposed by Exeter. Yet his remarks were underscored by his bad memories of a social environment where cliquish fraternity life ruled

all organizations and societies. Ultimately, he concluded, responsibility for both the good and the bad
rested with Perry, "a pleasant but bumbling presence."

Another student in the late twenties recalls a minor
liability of Dr. Perry's:

> I spoke only once in three years to the most dis-
> tinguished person in the school, Lewis Perry, the
> Principal, and that was under trying circum-
> stances in his office, when, under the prod of my
> mother's letters, he tried to come to grips with me
> over my most notable shortcomings. He seemed
> to hate the effort as much as I did, and he quite
> botched it.

Two years later Dean Wells Kerr would have handled
the situation with firmness and dispatch.

Critics also saw in Perry an indecisiveness that
probably stemmed from his inborn kindness. He
found it very difficult to fire anyone, and at times he
was too patient with mediocre performance.

All these criticisms were heard from time to time,
and they cannot be simply dismissed. But they repre-
sent a distinctly minority viewpoint. Without offering
excessive praise, let me just say that as the reputation
of Phillips Exeter Academy steadily grew, Lewis
Perry was generally deemed the major reason why,
and his own standing in the national educational
community rose appropriately.

Perry's life, however, was not bounded totally by
the world of Phillips Exeter. In 1922, when Deerfield

Academy was undergoing a desperate struggle for its life, he hurried to endorse the school, writing, "I know of no school in the country which I believe in more thoroughly than I do in the Deerfield Academy." And he was equally enthusiastic about the still-young Frank Boyden, who was to become a lifelong friend. Together with Al Stearns and Horace Taft, Perry raised $300,000, and Deerfield carried on.

Perry's family life remained as rich as ever. Although Margaret suffered several miscarriages, ten years after Lewis, Jr., was born came Emily Perry (now Cox). As her arrival became imminent, Margaret, her sister Juliette, and Mrs. Emily Russell conspired to get Perry out of the way by sending him to a Red Sox baseball game. Emily was her father's delight and recalls how from her youngest days he used to read aloud to her and give her violets on her birthday. Like her older brother, Emily, too, became a school principal, presiding skillfully over the destinies of the Exeter Day School.

One of the remarkable sides to Perry was his friendship with so many of the men who made fortunes in "The Golden Twenties." His relationships with George A. Plimpton, '73 (publisher); Jeremiah Smith, Jr., '88 (lawyer); William Boyce Thompson, '90 (copper magnate); James N. Hill, '89 (railroad executive); Thomas W. Lamont, '88 (banker); and especially Edward S. Harkness, a graduate of St. Paul's School, who made his fortune in oil, resulted in very substantial additions to the school's endowment and to its physical plant. Perry was not a businessman, but his very naïveté in money matters seemed to endear him to those whose fortunes were riding high before the crash of the stock market in 1929.

Jeremiah Smith, Jr., a trustee of the academy since 1907 and president of the trustees, 1920–1925, was in 1920 made League of Nations High Commissioner for Hungary, then in hopeless financial condition. Nicknamed Hungary's Yankee Godfather, he lived simply, refused a salary of $100,000 and a fancy car, and by the use of good old-fashioned horse sense put the country back on its feet. His dealings were so open and aboveboard that the expression "It's Jerry" came to mean "It's on the level."

Late in 1928 Perry wrote a long letter to copper magnate Colonel Thompson, another trustee of the academy, noting Andover's celebration of its 150th birthday with endowment for ten professorships, mostly "through the amazing activity of Tom Cochran." He listed what he thought were Exeter's greatest needs:

1. Endowment for teachers' salaries
2. A science laboratory
3. A covered Cage (winter track and baseball)
4. An addition to the Graduates' House
5. An administration building
6. A big room for reading and conversation.

He concluded, "I am writing this letter merely to show you what we are trying to do." A little more than a year later, on January 28, 1930, Perry, then in London on a visit to British schools, received a cablegram from Jeremiah Smith, Jr., which said:

Yesterday Colonel Thompson gave Exeter one million dollars cash following idea he long had in mind. Gift to be used as Trustees think best, but Thompson thinks more attention could be given educating boys in a scientific way and possibly some could be applied in that direction. He also feels a good deal of care should be used in handling seemingly backward boys who might thereby get through successfully. He especially feels first year hardest. He also thinks apart from academic questions a better hotel should be put up in Exeter. Lamont and I feel it desirable that this gift should be kept absolutely quiet until after your return. You can tell Rogers and Delano asking them to communicate it to no one. Assume you will wish to cable Thompson regarding this magnificent gift. . . . Isn't it wonderful!

Thus Thompson, who fifteen years before had given the new gymnasium and swimming pool, now expressed his confidence in both Perry and the school by a gift which provided a new science building, a much-needed administration building, a baseball cage, and (with the help of his family) a new inn.

Perry's list of successes was growing. But it was a long time before he could enjoy them. For on December 28, 1928, he suffered one of the great tragedies of his life when Margaret Hubbell Perry died after a long illness. The loss was heartbreaking not only to her family but to the whole community. Years later, writing to a friend who had lost his wife, Perry said, "Having known something about sorrow myself, I can only tell you that work is the greatest possible help. I am always a little sorry for people who have to go to the ends of the earth to try to escape sorrow."

He survived the loss with only the greatest difficulty. Harris Thomas, a close friend on the faculty, later recalled:

> He was a stricken—a broken, despondent, almost desperate man. . . . He could not summon the courage to see people; he could not face the school, especially at morning Chapel, and he wept constantly. His doctor said in effect, "This will pass. You will persevere. You will recover in time." To Lewis' surprise, and without knowing how or why, it did pass. The sense of loss remained with him but there seemed to have been added to his character an increased sympathy and understanding. He emerged serene and confident, not immune to human suffering, but willing and able to face it and triumph.

Margaret was survived by her husband and her two children, Lewis, Jr., and Emily, and by her two sisters, Mrs. Mason Adams and Mrs. Robert Derby. Seven years later Dr. Perry was to marry Juliette Adams, his sister-in-law, who had lost her husband. In the meantime, Sherwood Smedley, a member of the Exeter Science Department, and his wife, Dorothy, Williamstown cousins of Perry's, moved into the principal's house to assist with the care of the children, then fifteen and five years of age, and to manage the housekeeping and the minimal but necessary entertaining. They were succeeded in this capacity by Mrs. Sarah Pierce.

Among the many letters of condolence Perry received was one from his friend George Catlett Marshall, Jr., who had served as a colonel on General John Pershing's staff and accompanied him on visits to his son at Exeter. From Fort Benning Marshall wrote:

> You have all my sympathy and my prayers for a little ease of your suffering. I can understand somewhat of what you now endure and my heart goes out to you. Fortunately you are blessed with a fine son and a delightful daughter.

The letter concluded with an invitation to rest at Marshall's home. As he grew older, Perry often spoke of Marshall as the person he most admired.

Another of his heroes was Dr. Harvey Cushing, an eminent surgeon at the Peter Bent Brigham Hospital in Boston. Dr. Cushing had a summer home at Little Boar's Head, near Rye, New Hampshire, and he, too, helped Perry through the lonely years following Margaret's death.

THE HARKNESS PLAN

$\sim\!\!\!\!\xi\}\!\!\sim$

WHAT BECAME known as the Harkness Plan resulted from thirty years of friendship between the gregarious Lewis Perry and the shy, modest Edward S. Harkness. Their chance meeting in 1902 led to a mutual interest in the theater, and they shared many vacations together, including some at Yeamans Hall near Charleston, South Carolina, one of their favorite winter haunts. The Perrys often celebrated the Fourth of July at the Harkness summer home in Goshen Point, New London, Connecticut.

Harkness's oil interests had made him a multimillionaire. Yet when the two dined or went to the theater, Perry was just as likely as Harkness to pay the bill. Indeed, Perry seldom asked him directly for money, although Harkness had made several large gifts to Exeter. And Harkness found this attitude exceptional, to say the least. Once, Perry told me, Harkness burst out on their way home from the theater: "Dammit, Lewis, don't you know I have money? Everyone else asks for it; why don't you? Do you want to know why I love you more than any man

I have ever known? You were such a damn fool, you didn't know that I had money!"

Harkness, a graduate of St. Paul's and Yale, had given substantially to Harvard and Yale. He had visited Exeter several times during the 1920s and in May 1928 donated to both Exeter and Andover $320,-000 to establish professorships. In addition, he gave smaller amounts for buildings. Now he wrote to Perry, "If you will get up a scheme, I'll give you all the money you need to put it into operation."

In September 1929 Harkness and Perry met, and Harkness spoke of what he was doing for Harvard in terms of the so-called House Plan, adding that if Exeter would conceive a similar proposal for teaching, he would support it. Perry could barely contain his enthusiasm and on October 2 wrote to Harkness that the opportunity could mean more "not only for Exeter, but for secondary education in general than has ever been done before. I doubt whether any school in the world has had the chance that seems now to have come to us."

On October 11 Perry reported to the trustees that the proposition was potentially "the greatest gain the school has ever made. . . . The possibilities of Mr. Harkness' proposal are staggering."

Jeremiah Smith, Jr., president of the trustees, was also in close touch with Harkness, to whom he was grateful for several reasons. First, of course, was the plan itself. Second, Harkness had provided funds for Lewis Perry and George B. Rogers to visit British public schools, a trip which, in Smith's words, "will be of great value to them and to Exeter, and I hope in time to all secondary schools, both public and private." Most of all, Smith appreciated that the projects had brought Perry out of the depression he had suffered after Margaret's death. Again in Smith's words, "[They have] given Lewis a new lease on life and a new interest. I haven't seen him more alert, mentally interested and enthusiastic about anything, nor in better condition, since his return from Europe in the summer of 1928 before Margaret was taken ill."

The visit to British schools, which would so influence the formation of the Harkness Plan, took place between January and March 1930. Perry and Rogers were received by the headmasters and talked with students, masters, and "old boys." They did not visit classes, but they observed headmasters at work and especially enjoyed their stays with Rendall of Winchester and Malim of Wellington. They talked as well at Oxford with Sir Richard Livingston, the head of Corpus Christi College and a leading philosopher of education, to whom they had carried a letter of introduction from Thomas W. Lamont.

In all, they visited many schools, including Winchester, Eton, St. Paul's, Merchant Taylor's, St. Andrew's, Wellington, Harrow, Rugby, and Oundle, and were much impressed by what they saw. What intrigued them most about the British institutions was their flexibility; their house plans; their attention to art, music, and shopwork; their emphasis on games, religion, the classics, and character; and especially their use of the sixth form, or twelfth grade, as a year of advanced concentration in a preferred field of study. Oddly enough, with all their inquiries about English schools, not a single person asked about Exeter!

The trip concluded with an "at home" at Lord and Lady Astor's Clivedon, several evenings in the theater, and a voyage home on the *Europa* beginning March 20, 1930. After they arrived home, Rogers wrote a full report that was used in formulating the Harkness Plan.

However, on March 31 Harkness turned down Exeter's initial plan for use of his prospective gift. The scheme seemed too indefinite, and Harkness challenged Perry to do better. He did not tread gently, either, chiding Perry and the faculty firmly:

> What are the outstanding benefits you expect to derive from this plan? To what extent and in what way is secondary school education in this country going to be benefitted by this plan? What is to be the size of the classes you will have? Just how is the tutorial system to function—and exactly how many instructors will you require to operate it? What will be the actual amounts needed?
>
> When you went abroad I had hoped that you would come home with several suggestions of a fundamental nature that were so sweeping and so different from methods prevailing here that one could see at a glance that were they adopted, the whole educational system in our secondary schools would not only be changed, but changed

enormously for the better. I have yet been unable
to get my teeth into anything that promises great
fundamental benefits to our educational system.

Thus inspired, Perry and his close advisers (Rogers,
Frank Cushwa, Corning Benton, Wells Kerr, and Jeremiah Smith) went back to work. Between March 31
and October 30, 1930, they delineated in much greater
detail the school's participation in the great experiment.

The central group was an intriguing mixture of
personalities. Rogers was the philosopher: deliberate,
analytical, and of a decidedly liberal bent. Cushwa was
the dynamic teacher: vital, with a gift for great laughter and for life itself. Corning Benton was the treasurer
of the academy: a tireless worker, well-read historian,
skilled carpenter, and inveterate punster. Wells Kerr
was the first dean of the academy: a lifelong bachelor,
with a most felicitous manner, but capable of enormous depth of feeling. Every faculty member was
brought into their discussions. And finally there was
Smith, president of the trustees, who has been described earlier. Leading these men, all full partners
in the formulation of policy, was Perry.

On October 30, 1930, Perry wrote Harkness a long
letter, reprinted in the Appendix of this book, explain-
ing in detail what came to be known as the Harkness
Plan. What were its elements? Briefly stated, the plan
emphasized the individual student and had as one of
its major goals the stimulation of his natural curiosity.
Class size would be cut from twenty-five or thirty to
ten or twelve. These students, grouped roughly ac-

cording to ability, would sit with their teacher around
an oval table, looking at one another's faces rather
than at the backs of one another's necks. Conversation
and discussion, not lecture, would be the order. The
plan provided for new buildings, most notably Phillips
Hall, as well as for twenty-five more teachers to be
added to the faculty over a period of three years.
More than half the Harkness gift endowed the salaries
of these new instructors. With the increased faculty,
individual teachers would have fewer students to ad-
vise and counsel in the school's dormitories and houses
and could thereby offer closer individual attention.

At the heart of the Harkness Plan was quality teaching. Perry and Harkness put brains ahead of bricks.
And the result of their efforts was a dramatically improved school, in which learning proceeded more
effectively than ever before at the 150-year-old academy.

At the end of his letter Perry listed the "Final Estimate of Cost":

1)	Reconstruction of four dormi- tories (Abbot, Soule, Hoyt, Peabody)	$ 250,000
2)	Removal and re-equipping wooden houses	50,000
3)	Alteration of four other dormi- tories (Amen, Cilley, Went- worth, and Webster)	20,000
4)	Construction of four new houses, including $125,000 for cost of dining halls	925,000

5) Reconstruction and furnishing of recitation rooms in the Academy Building	30,000
6) Board for new instructors and families	400,000
7) Construction of wings of Academy Building	150,000
8) Construction of one new study-conference building	315,000
9) Capitalization of the salaries of three instructors for sabbatical years	300,000
10) Endowment of salaries of 25 additional teachers	3,000,000
11) Maintenance fund for new buildings	400,000
	$5,840,000

Barely one week later Harkness replied with a very brief letter that contained this thrilling news:

I have been greatly interested in reading your letter of October 30th. The plan discussed therein for changing the method of teaching and housing at Exeter coincides with my ideas and the offer I am about to make is based on this plan as described.

The total estimate for the cost of carrying out your scheme amounts to $5,840,000 and I note that the School considers this a final estimate and will stand back of it. With this understanding, I shall be glad to contribute the above-mentioned amount, namely, Five Million Eight Hundred

Forty Thousand Dollars ($5,840,000) payable in
cash or securities (at the then market value) or
both, as I may desire.

Had it not been for the long friendship and complete trust that existed between Harkness and Perry,
the gift would never have been made. Exeter received
the money because Harkness knew Perry would spend
it wisely. And it was this capacity for friendship, this
ability to maintain trust, that made Lewis Perry what
he was.

The gift was made public in mid-November 1930,
and Perry wrote to Harkness on November 21:

Letters have been coming in all day by the
score in regard to your magnificent gift. I got all
the faculty together Tuesday night and with
much applause, and every man on his feet, they
pledged themselves to carry this on.

Now the years between 1930 and 1940 would be spent
in the exciting work of selecting new faculty members, making physical improvements required by the
plan, and sharing with others the new opportunities
and demands of secondary school teaching.

These new faculty members, appointed in the early
1930s, came to Exeter from a great variety of schools
and colleges. Most were experienced teachers in their
late twenties or early thirties. Perry was an excellent
judge of men, and his interviews, though informal,
allowed him to perceive people accurately, and he had
a way of finding lively, determined, competent teachers.

Some of the appointments were a direct result of Perry's wide-ranging inquiries and accurate "rifle shots," while other applicants, hearing of the Harkness Plan, simply were able to meet the competition. Many, of course, came because of Perry's contagious enthusiasm for the future of the school. But no doubt they were also attracted by the modest teaching load and the new physical arrangements in the classroom, where seminar tables helped to break down the institutional curse. Each teacher had his own room, nicely decorated with curtains, ample bookcases, bulletin boards, magazines on the table, and pictures on the wall. Many rooms even had open fireplaces. Each classroom, which also served as office and conference area, became the personal study of the man who used it, an extension of his personality.

Some older teachers, conditioned by larger classes and earlier methods, still lectured or conducted recitations, but Perry reminded all the faculty of the skills necessary for seminar classes and encouraged the new kind of teaching and learning made possible by the new buildings. The impact on students was immediate. They worked just as hard, but in a different way: less in order to memorize and recite, more in order to express opinions and raise questions.

By the mid-thirties the plan was in full effect. The costs of building were declining, and a part of the Harkness gift was returned to the donor. The individual student had become the focus, and the principal never let the faculty forget it.

Perry was celebrating his seventeenth year as principal, but surely no words from those years pleased

him as much as this minute in the faculty meeting on
November 25, 1930:

> Mr. Jeremiah Smith, Jr., President of the
> Trustees, spoke to the faculty about the Harkness
> gift to the Academy. The following resolution
> was adopted by vote of the Faculty:
>
> "The Principal and Faculty of the Phillips
> Exeter Academy express hereby their deep and
> honest gratitude to Mr. Edward S. Harkness for
> the great gift he has so generously bestowed
> upon the school.
>
> "Hardly less significant than the specific re-
> form in methods of instruction is the encourage-
> ment which this benefaction gives to fresher ef-
> fort and wider views in the great business of
> education, to the reexamination of accepted aims,
> the thoughtful adjustment of new means to ends,
> and to the conscious and inspiring fellowship of
> many laboring together for a single cause. What-
> ever may be the outcome, this school at least, it
> may be reasonably hoped, will henceforth be a
> better place for the eager and enquiring, and even
> for the vagrant and reluctant mind of youth."

And how appropriate it was that as the school was
about to celebrate its 150th anniversary, the Harkness
Plan would be instituted, inaugurating a new era of
education at Exeter.

YEARS OF DECISION
1933–1940
◈

For Lewis Perry the thirties were years of deep satisfaction, difficult decision, and distressing loss. The Harkness Plan was under way, with great success. He was most flattered to be offered the presidency of Williams College and thought seriously about accepting the position. Yet in these years his life was diminished not only by the death of Margaret but by the passing of many relatives, friends, and colleagues.

The progress of the Harkness Plan was a source of great satisfaction. One immediate result of its implementation was a sharp lowering of the attrition rate in the school. In a community of 750 students of most varied backgrounds, living under high standards of academic performance and conduct, as few as 15 boys a year were asked to leave. In the twenties the rate had been five or six times that high. But now every boy knew he had someone to turn to, someone who knew him well and could help in a difficult moment. Furthermore, amid smaller classes and because of the closer relationship between adviser and student, the boys who were experiencing problems could be recog-

The editorial board of The Lawrence, the Lawrenceville School student paper, 1894. Lewis Perry, second from left, was managing editor at seventeen.

A Perry family portrait, about 1910. In the front row, left to right, Grace Perry and Mary Smedley Perry; in the back row, Arthur, Walter, Lewis, Bliss, and Carroll Perry.

From left to right, Lewis Perry, George Eastman, Charles A. Lindbergh, Thomas A. Edison, Henry Ford, and President Stratton of MIT at a meeting called by Edison in 1927 to encourage promising young men to pursue careers in science.

Dr. Perry with E. S. Wells Kerr, 1931

At commencement exercises, 1946

Dr. Perry with his successor, William G. Saltonstall, 1946.

Percy Rogers, far left, with Saltonstall and Perry, 1946.

Dr. Perry (seated) with three principals: from left to right, Richard W. Day, Saltonstall, and W. Ernest Gillespie, 1964.

nized much more quickly. They were not lost in the bustle of school life.

Those on the faculty, which I joined in 1932 as a member of the History Department and as one of the first appointees under the Harkness Plan, were gratified on several counts. We recognized an upward trend in academic grades as well as an improved college admissions record and better performances in college by graduates. But what pleased us most was our absolute conviction that each individual student was growing up in a community of high standards. We saw no loss of the students' valued independence. Each individual was responsible for taking his own life in hand and making something of it.

W. S. Gifford, '35, wrote about his experience in the Harkness system from the students' point of view. He praised its ideals but contrasted their practice in one class and their absence in others. He emphasized as well an important point about the nature and demands of the system:

> To me the success of the conference in superseding the recitation depends ultimately on one factor, the professors. For no matter whether the tables are round or square, if the professor of a class is dull, uninspiring, uninterested in his work, the spirit of the class will be that old, mechanical, plodding recitation.

Perry was aware of that. He knew his main job was to make strong appointments to the faculty. Yet his interviews with candidates appeared almost casual, and sometimes he never even mentioned salary or teaching load. But he knew people and recognized quality, and by making decisions in conjunction with his department chairmen and senior colleagues, he made few mistakes.

In only one area did he hesitate. That was in choosing teachers for science and mathematics, in which he relied heavily on the advice of John Hogg and Philip Hulburd. However secure he might have been as principal, he never quite overcame his old uncertainties about those subjects.

Like any man who stays for so long at the heart of an institution, Perry became an institution himself. Most of us remember him in the 1930s by his regular attendance at early-morning chapel. His delightful Bible readings and prayers alternated with favorites like "The Devil and Daniel Webster," the mob scene in *Huckleberry Finn*, Leacock's "My First Day at the Bank," and excerpts from *Life with Father*. At these times his lifelong study of public speaking and drama stood him well. He could "play" on the audience of 750 students as an organist plays on his instrument.

His voice was deep and mellifluous, a comforting voice with a resonant timbre that could always be heard, although he never seemed to yell. But his most effective technique was the pause, that extra hesitation before the moment of surprise or humor.

Not all his readings were humorous, however. Many students recall his keeping them abreast of the world by reading editorials from the *New York Times*. And morning chapel always ended with a prayer. Yet even such a moment allowed for schoolboy humor. His favorite, some said his only, prayer, ended with the familiar line "And so bring us to the end of the day unashamed and with a quiet mind." The whole back of the room would say it with him in unison, and if Perry heard it, he never mentioned it. In Phillips Church he kept a large-type copy of the Lord's Prayer in his hymnal. A boy discovered it and commented in the hymnal, "For Christ's sakes, Lew, why don't you learn this thing by heart?"

As principal Perry wanted a sense of the whole student body, its ideas and feelings, and he kept in touch as best he could through weekly dinners with the Student Council. These were referred to as "Perry's smiling steak-eaters," because the menu kept the boys "happy and submissive."

In an effort to keep in touch with the individual boys and give them encouragement, Perry often asked a few to "remain after chapel." On one occasion he asked a brilliant student, "Are you getting any Bs?" (B was considered a high mark in those days.) The straight-A student said he was not. "Well," said Perry, "I'll be seeing you again next term and hope by then you'll be getting a B." When the boy was interviewed a couple of months later, one A had indeed dropped to a B. Dr. Perry asked him the same question. "Are you getting any Bs?"

"Yes," the boy admitted. "One."

"Good," said Perry. "Keep it up." A student of this period looks back on him as "a complete charmer and the greatest bluffer who ever lived."

Perry sometimes admonished himself for his frequent absences from Exeter, and he was not alone in doing so. Some faculty members regarded him as an

absentee principal who did not know what was going
on when he was at the Tavern Club in Boston or the
Century Association in New York. Somehow he always seemed to have time and seldom gave the appearance of working very hard, and therefore to some
he appeared "profoundly lazy." Yet he had the knack
of inspiring others to work. Furthermore, he knew
how to pace himself and came back from meetings
more able to deal with problems than if he had not
gone away. As he wrote to his brother Walter, "[The
school] seems to go better when . . . other people are
doing the job. I have a sneaking suspicion that perhaps it does go better when I'm not around. It's a
solemn thought, and I do not let myself dwell on it."

But in 1933 Perry did have cause to sit back and
reflect on his years at Exeter. The Harkness Plan was
under way, to virtually universal approval. The spirit
of the school was strong, its reputation equally strong
and growing. And Perry, now approaching the twentieth anniversary of his appointment, had a right to
look back in pride.

In the same year his Williams classmates asked him
once more to accept the presidency of the Class of
1898. "You have long been our informal and unani-
mous choice as leader and spokesman." The offer was
flattering, but a far more serious and more consequen-
tial one would soon have to be weighed.

In 1934 Perry faced that crucial decision when
President Harry R. Garfield of Williams retired. The
trustees' first choice as his successor was Professor
James Phinney Baxter, Harvard historian, but he had

just been made master of Adams House at Harvard and felt he could not leave.

The trustees then urged Perry to consider the post. The temptation to accept must have been strong, for Williams was his home and his college, and for thirteen years he had been a member of the faculty. Everyone at Exeter knew he was facing a dilemma.

His correspondence gives some notion of the pressures he felt that spring. To Mrs. James (Emily) Russell, an old friend, he wrote on April 8, 1934:

> Harry Garfield and my brother Bliss made it about as difficult as possible as they took the ground that it was my duty to go to Williams. I was an old Williams man, all my family connections were with Williams, and now they need someone like me, who knows all the alumni and could pull the thing together. I was surprised at my brother Bliss and also my sister Grace, for I thought they would say "Stay at Exeter," but they were very keen to have me go to Williams.

We all heaved a mighty sigh of relief when he decided to remain as principal. One reason for his decision, as he wrote to Arthur Perry, Bliss's son and headmaster of Milton Academy, was his desire to continue his work at Exeter, to consolidate the Harkness Plan. Other possible reasons appear to have been his age, fifty-seven, and his desire to work with young people of high school rather than college age. Moreau Delano, his old friend from Lawrenceville, and Thomas W. Lamont, president of Exeter's trustees, were among the many who wrote to offer approval of his choice.

Perry's own tongue-in-cheek response about the matter to his friend Ruth Kellogg, is characteristically Perry:

> I had the chance to go up to Williamstown this spring as President, but as you and Harry weren't able to make me President of Harvard I decided I was in a resentful mood and decided to live out my life here in New Hampshire. If you and Harry haven't enough influence to make me the head of Harvard, what good is friendship, anyway?

So Perry remained on the job at Exeter. But the drama with Williams was not yet played out. Although he refused the presidency of the college, Perry was elected a trustee in 1934 and therefore was closely involved with the selection of the next president, Tyler Dennett, who had been professor of international relations at Princeton. The college may have needed a shaking up, as Perry himself wrote in 1935 to Damon Hall, a Boston lawyer: "I rather think we need a Theodore Roosevelt in the quiet Berkshire Valley." But Perry and Dennett were soon to be at loggerheads.

Perry tried to support Dennett initially, as the new president sought a more diverse student body at Williams, less sophisticated and more heterogeneous. Dennett saw too few blacks and other ethnic minorities and minced no words in saying so. Indeed, it was to a degree his manner rather than his programs that aroused resentment from so many sources, as Perry indicated in that same letter to Hall: "He is a tactless fellow who doesn't take advice and who is likely to make a major blunder at any time."

But Dennett's arguments about minorities struck a nerve in Perry, especially in conjunction with an article published the same year in *Fortune* magazine. The piece criticized private schools for their failure to produce more public servants from their often wealthy clientele. Perry reacted sharply to the attack, pointing out that 25 percent of Exeter's students were on scholarship and that full-pay boys paid only about one-half what it cost the school to educate them.

Nevertheless, the question of minority representation at Exeter was a sensitive one. Blacks had attended Exeter long before Perry's time and done well. As late as March 1938, however, he wrote to Vernon Munroe to explain his worries about "colored boys" in Exeter and what he felt was their "social loneliness." He quoted Booker T. Washington's advice to Al Stearns that it would be "a great mistake for colored boys to come to either Exeter or Andover." Perry went so far as to say, "I am sure that a colored boy is hurt rather than helped by his entrance into Exeter."

Even within the context of his day this was a blind spot. While it may not be fair to judge a person by the standards of a different age, Perry denied Exeter's democratic tradition in permitting limits on the numbers of blacks and Jews in the academy. He never specifically discussed quotas of any kind, but he did suggest that limits were advisable. He invariably treated individual blacks and other minority members with utmost courtesy, but at the same time he thought

the school "had to be careful in regard to Jews," although "some of the best boys have been Jews." Furthermore, Perry's active role in his Williams fraternity
may have caused him to postpone the abolition of fraternities at Exeter. It was not until the early forties
that a faculty committee I chaired unanimously recommended their elimination, a move which aided the
school enormously.

But what most irritated Perry about Dennett was a
speech to Williams alumni in Boston in 1937, when
the president commented, in what he thought was an
aside, that Williams enrolled too many "nice boys"
(meaning independent school boys). The press played
up this statement and turned it into the "nice boy
controversy." Perry was on the telephone to Dennett
the next day, and he was angry. And he followed the
telephone call with a letter:

> With your desire to have more public school
> boys in Williams I am entirely in sympathy.
> . . . If you would take my advice you would
> bear down on the fact that you want more high
> school boys at Williams and let it go at that. You
> are in no position to be God Almighty and give
> your opinion in public of the relative merits of
> different schools. . . . I know exactly what you
> want—the fine, rugged, unsophisticated country
> boy who thirty years ago used to reach the cam-
> pus of a New England college, put his carpet bag
> down, and say, "I want an education." Well,
> Henry Ford and the radio have just about elimi-
> nated that type of boy.

Dennett resigned in 1937, and Perry made this observation:

> The trouble was this. Tyler Dennett, with all his good qualities, has taken some leaves out of the book of Hitler and Mussolini and was anxious to be more or less of a dictator . . . he wanted the power of veto over the actions of the Board of Trustees. . . . He was temperamentally unfitted to be the head of a college like Williams.

Perry drafted a resolution of thanks to Dennett on behalf of the trustees, then turned his attention to selecting a new president.

James Phinney Baxter and Perry were the leading candidates, but most trustees, including Perry, saw Baxter as the logical choice. And this time he did accept the position, to Perry's great pleasure.

It was while Perry was under pressure as a Williams trustee and possible president that he was named in 1936 as the first recipient of the college's Rogerson Cup, "each year given to an alumnus in recognition of service and loyalty to the college and of distinction in some field of endeavour." Rogerson and Perry had been close friends, and in making the award, President Dennett spoke of Perry "whose service and loyalty to the College are as little in question as are his achievements in education."

It was one of many honors that were coming to Perry. In May 1934 the faculty celebrated his twentieth anniversary at Exeter. George Rogers, a Williams alumnus and senior member of the faculty, was the main speaker, and he summed up Perry's gift. His genius, Rogers said, was:

> . . . his belief, both reasoned and instinctive, that of all things in this world the one of greatest importance is a human being. Each person has his essential worth, is different from all others, and deserves respect, perhaps affection.

On June 25, 1935, Perry suddenly left the Exeter commencement exercises early for "an important engagement," as he put it. In the last few months, encouraged by a cheering section of his children, nieces, and friends, he had become engaged to Juliette Hubbell Adams at the suggestion of Ruth Derby, her sister. His initial response to Ruth: "Now I know that you really are crazy." Nevertheless, soon afterward he wrote Juliette in Milton, proposing marriage. That night, when "Mag" Adams, Juliette's daughter, and some friends returned from a party, she told them of Perry's proposal, and they exulted. The next day she called him at his office: "I accept."

Letters, telephone calls, and flowers followed. "Are you really going to marry that spitfire?" one friend exclaimed. On April 25 Perry wrote his friend Drury, "The children are in seventh heaven of joy. I know that this is about the rightest thing I've ever done!"

So it was that he drove directly from Exeter's commencement exercises to the Chapel of the New Jerusalem at Little Harbor, Portsmouth. Bishop John Dallas of New Hampshire, assisted by Carroll Perry, married them. The congregation consisted of Perry's children, Lewis, Jr., and Emily, and Juliette's daughter, Mag.

For their honeymoon the Perrys went to England. As they boarded the ship for Southampton, Perry warned Juliette, "I am a strange man on a boat. I like to be alone, not meet a lot of people, just sort of stay by myself and do some reading." After a day or so Juliette noticed that such was not precisely the case. He was on such friendly terms with the steward who brought up breakfast and had such intense philosophical discussions with him that Juliette could not get up to get dressed. And when they got to London, Perry had to stay at a particular hotel because the doorman there was such a good friend of his.

While there, Juliette saw an old friend who did not know that she had remarried. "What are you doing here?" the friend asked.

"I'm traveling with Dr. Perry."

It was a long and very happy marriage.

During the seven lonely years of Perry's widowerhood he had grown especially close to his children. In spite of the absence of their mother, they grew up happy and successful. Lewis was graduated from Harvard in 1936, then spent two years at New College, Oxford, which his father enjoyed vicariously. On October 20, 1936, Perry wrote to his son, in words that reflected his own growth and sympathies:

Most of the Perrys are slow developers, and I think in some ways it may be a good thing. I know I did not get a real intellectual interest in things until the middle of my sophomore year in college. I think all of us are dependent on responsibilities to wake us up.

Another letter from father to son reflects Perry's own intrinsic optimism:

Get a lot of exercise in Oxford, good sleep, and keep a clear conscience. I think I get more religious as I get older. A great many of the people who break down haven't the right philosophy of life. They have lost faith in everything and when they look around find very little to live for. You couldn't have a better model in everything than Uncle Bliss—calm, steady, hopeful, and understanding.

It interests me that you can enjoy yourself while you are alone. I have always been that way. If you have books to read you are not alone, anyway.

After his study at New College, young Lew became a member of the faculty at Lawrenceville School, as his father had been thirty-nine years before. The appointment delighted both. Perry congratulated his son on the fine salary—"fifteen hundred and your living. By Jove, that's great!"

Nothing could have pleased Perry more than that his son was given his old room. Lew served Lawrenceville well for many years before going to Colorado Springs, where, until 1978, he served as headmaster of Fountain Valley School.

One love both Perrys shared throughout their lives was the art of public speaking. Professor Packard, teacher of public speaking at Harvard, had compared them, as father wrote to son on March 22, 1937:

Packard congratulated me on my speech and said that my rate was perfect. He said that at first you were inclined to talk a little too fast. I can't tell you what a thrill it gave me to have you and me compared as speakers by an expert.

Perry himself remained in constant demand as a speaker. One place to which he returned regularly was Deerfield, where at commencement a large dinner was traditionally held, attended by 1,000 or so students, faculty, parents, friends, and local citizens. For years the celebration took place in a tent, later in a new gymnasium. Distinguished speakers were among the sixty to eighty head-table guests, and Perry always presided over the festivities. If a big-name speaker dropped the ball, Perry would pick it up, treat the crowd to a few stories, then say, "Before I give out the prizes, we want you all to know that we love those who get no prizes." After the clearing of the dishes and the singing of "America the Beautiful," Perry would say, "And now we're about to start the dinner, if anyone can find Dr. Boyden," who was usually away from the head table, going the rounds and greeting friends. At one of these dinners in the new gym Perry looked up at the bare girders overhead and remarked, "About five thousand dollars, and next year we'll have a ceiling." And have one they did!

These dinners, over which Perry presided for forty years, probably saw him at his relaxed best. He loved going to them, and the dinners would have been incomplete without him. He also helped Dr. Boyden by becoming a trustee of Deerfield. Whenever a controversial matter was coming before the board, Boyden would brief Perry ahead of time, and Perry would say at the meeting, "Yes, Frank, you'd better go ahead and do it." It was difficult to deny him.

In 1939 Exeter celebrated Perry's twenty-fifth year as principal. His reaction was expressed in a letter to an old Philadelphia friend and alumnus:

> It doesn't seem to me as though I have been twenty-five years at Exeter. The time has gone so fast, and it still seems to me that I am a new man around here. . . . The only thing I can say for myself is that I have really tried. I think I have tried harder on this than on anything I have ever attempted, but of course anyone would have tried hard with such an opportunity.

But amid such celebration, as always, people mused about old age. Bliss, who had always thought his brother too social, urged him to cut down on activity. He even drew up for his brother a resolution, to be posted conspicuously:

> Out of deference to my family and to many friends who are seriously concerned about my health (though they lack the nerve to address me directly and tackle my brother Bliss instead) I make the following resolve. From this date until Easter vacation I will:
> 1) Cancel all speaking engagements
> 2) Cancel all committee meetings outside of Exeter

3) Allow myself not more than one dinner party
   a week, at home or abroad

4) Allow myself not more than one trip to Boston each week, preferably in the daytime.

Although Lewis's health was still good, Bliss's concerns were understandable. For the late thirties must
have been trying for Perry. Between 1936 and 1940
several old and close relatives and friends died: his
sister, Grace; his brothers Carroll and Arthur; Jimmy
Rogerson; Moreau Delano; Frank Cushwa; Joey Ford;
George B. Rogers, and, in 1940, Edward S. Harkness.
Perry never dwelt on these losses, but they were telling blows to him. He outlived these friends by thirty
years or more, but he never forgot them. To an extent
their places were taken by his closest advisers of the
last six years of his principalship—Wells Kerr, dean;
Ezra Pike Rounds, director of admissions; Myron
Williams, director of studies; Corning Benton, treasurer—and by many younger members of the faculty.

As World War II broke out, Perry urged the United
States to see the danger and to give prompt aid to
Britain. The Secondary School Defense League was
formed at Exeter in 1940 for the purpose of encouraging discussion, supporting a stronger national defense,
and promoting every possible aid to Britain. Perry was
soon a member of William Allen White's Committee
to Defend America by Aiding the Allies, and on October 8, 1940, he spoke on behalf of the White Committee in the Exeter Town Hall:

In the last twelve months you and I have
watched the fall of Poland, of Denmark, of Nor-

way, of Holland, of Belgium, of France, the en-
circlement of Sweden, the defeat and partition of
Finland, the partition of Rumania. Today we
watch the Battle of Britain. If Britain falls before
the Nazi drive for power we face a future more
critical than we have ever known since the country was founded.

We have got to light the flame and go crusad-
ing. We have got to be more dynamic than Hit-
ler. That should be easy. We are by nature a dynamic people, of an energy and vitality beside
which Nazism is a passing spasm.

If England falls we shall be alone in a hostile
world. . . . Rise up in wrath and demand that
we meet with full force, both physical and moral,
this menace to everything America stands for.

On November 4, 1940, Perry spoke in the same
spirit on radio station WRUL. He found secondary-
school students of that generation "stern realists, willing and eager to face facts. They merely recognize
that the history of the present and the future will have
to be written in steel rather than in words." And the
final words of his talk to graduating seniors in June,
1940, paid tribute to the

. . . splendidly given oration which Jim Conant, Jr. gave yesterday. Strength comes in trying hours. It has come to men who have made our
school. It will come, I believe, to you. Things in-
finitely precious to us are at stake. To win this
struggle which seems to be upon us we must call,
not on our lowest selves, but our higher selves.

The future will not care much about the things
this generation has *hated*. They will want to
know the things we *loved*, and here we can use
the old words which in the past ten years while
you were growing up have been used too seldom:
Let's come back to them—faith, truth, and freedom. And as a family let's not be afraid, for perfect love casteth out fear. Goodbye to you alumni.
We shall meet, I know, in happier days.

END OF AN ERA
1940–1946
❧§❧

ARLIER than most Americans, Lewis Perry recognized the fascist menace and took steps to see
the academy through World War II. "If I survive this
war," he wrote to his brother Walter, "I will be one
of the few headmasters in the country who has gone
through two wars. That's something, even though I
have not carried a gun or flown a plane." Like many
of us on the faculty who did enter the service, he saw
it as a war between freedom and slavery. He was reluctantly understanding as he saw thirty-four faculty
members go off to fight, but he felt strongly the need
for schools like Exeter to go on doing their job.

These years may have been his greatest. His steady-
ing influence on boys, faculty, and parents was felt
by everyone connected with the school. He was larger
than life in these late years, a symbol of continuity
and tradition, something for us to believe in. Although he himself did not serve, he did not simply sit.
He became chairman of the Preparatory School Committee for the Care of European Children, formed the
Secondary School Defense League, and spoke for Rus-

sian war relief. He saw to it that Exeter became the wartime home of many British boys and supported universal military training as a "regrettable necessity." Although not a strong supporter of President Roosevelt, Perry backed his foreign policy, including the early delivery of destroyers to Britain.

In December 1941, in response to questions from parents about the role of a school like Exeter in wartime, Perry wrote a long letter which affirmed his own beliefs in education, no matter what the crises of the day. And as he had during World War I, he warned against hasty decisions by boys eager to join the service. He stated:

> Hard, honest work in school and abundant physical exercise on the athletic field, under normal conditions and with an environment of congenial fellow students, should be the best possible preparation for whatever may come.

But running a school during wartime was not Perry's only task during these years. Other matters of exigency arose. The Supreme Court of New Hampshire decided in the academy's favor the long-standing tax case about whether the school's dormitories could be legally taxed. For many years the school had paid taxes to the town of Exeter under protest. Now town-gown relations became more strained than ever as the town was forced to pass a bond issue and raise the tax rate, and for a time Perry lost his close rapport with town officials. The following letter to Bliss reminds us that it was a bitter fight:

We have just won our tax case in the Supreme Court of New Hampshire. This means that our taxes are reduced $25,000 a year and that the town has to pay us back over $200,000 of back taxes. It will be a little hard for the town, but the town never lifted a finger when they knew that the selectmen were gouging us, and I think we shall now let the law take its course.

Another note, to Dudley Orr, an alumnus of Exeter and a Concord lawyer, was even more testy. It said in part:

. . . Now I suppose the town will want to have some meetings with us to see what we can do. Personally I feel a little hard-boiled on the matter. The town never made the slightest gesture when we were the underdog, and they let the selectmen soak us to the limit, so now I am in favor of letting the law take its course. I want to be fair, but I do not want to be easy.

In late 1944 Perry faced another agonizing moment. Dean Wells Kerr, his right-hand man, was offered the post of dean of the college at Princeton by his old friend President Harold Dodds. Kerr had served as secretary of the faculty and chairman of the Executive Committee and through both capacities dealt directly with every boy and every teacher in the school. Had he left, less than two years before Perry's own retirement and during the turmoil of war, it would have been a body blow to the school. Kerr eventually refused the offer, and Perry called the decision deserving of a "hallelujah." As Perry's successor I found Wells invaluable during my first seven years as principal. And it was he who later suggested I write this sketch of his closest friend.

Life for students at Exeter during the war years was as turbulent as it was for Perry and the faculty. *A Separate Peace*, the novel by John Knowles, an undergraduate during the war years, is set against that time, and Perry thought the portrait most accurate.

Whatever his burdens, Perry the principal never supplanted Perry the man. My wife and I saw a good deal of the Perrys in the summer of 1942, and with some reluctance he accepted my decision to go into the Naval Reserve. Still, he was confident and optimistic as usual and made clear that he hoped I would return to Exeter after the war had ended. He took a personal interest in our new home, finished that spring. To Bliss he wrote:

> Bill Saltonstall has got into his new house and already has a lovely garden out behind. He enjoys the work with rake and hoe. If I had only had that in my system, I would have gone far, but I hate it as much as ever.

No victory gardener he! But figuratively he gardened well, as this poem by his faculty colleague Chilson Leonard suggests:

The Grapevines on the Granite Rocks
for Lewis Perry

You were the sun that ripened grapes
On old New England vines;

Upon the classic rocks you shone
With their green tender lines.

You warmed the rocks, you warmed the leaves,
You watched the growing fruit;
You pruned excessive sprouts away.
You dug around the root.

Your grapes grew firmly ripe and sweet,
A few refused to jell,
But many we see in time became
Full-bodied wines, as well.

Always Perry found time for humor and relaxation. As he wrote to his brother Bliss:

I'm going to play my first tennis of the year this afternoon. Katharyn Saltonstall and I are going to take on the Shaun Kellys. It makes me feel young just to think of getting on the tennis court [he was sixty-six at the time], but I don't believe I shall be very effective.

But pride is a funny thing. And Perry, who took such pleasure in tennis and who had played it virtually all his life, could not be satisfied with a mediocre performance. A year later he decided to give up the game:

I have retired from the courts. I can't bear to have the people sitting around the courts saying, "Isn't he wonderful for such an old man?" So I have retired gracefully like Gene Tunney. I am sorry we can't have some tennis matches next summer, but I guess that my retirement, unlike Adelina Patti's, will stick.

Perhaps it was this recognition of his own age, as well as the pressure of running the school during wartime, that led Perry to enjoy reminiscing, even reliving the past. In 1944, for instance, he wrote to Lieutenant (jg) Lewis Perry about the births of young Lew and Emily:

> I shall never forget March 4, 1913. That was the day Woodrow Wilson was inaugurated and the day you were born, a cold, rather blustery, snowy day, but a big day in my life. You have given me about the most pleasure I have ever received from anyone and someday when this damnable war is over we can go back and reminisce.
>
> I don't believe a mother ever loved a boy as much as Mother loved you, but she was quite wise about you just the same.

And on June 28, 1944:

> This is Emily's birthday. What a great day that was twenty-one years ago. . . . I have been a little ashamed of the fact that when Emily was born I was at a baseball game, but I remember the joy of seeing her when I got back. What a lovely girl she was, and I think now she is getting more beautiful all the time.

He felt great love for Margaret Peltz, his stepdaughter, and her sons, Toby and Willie, who lived with the Perrys during several of the war years. Toby's nickname for his stepgrandfather was Goo, and his grandmother Juicy. These names were as close as he could come to pronouncing Lew and Juliette!

As always he had trips to make, and Mrs. Perry made a point of getting in touch with her husband on Sunday nights when he was away. One Sunday she telephoned a telegraph message through an innocent and naïve New Hampshire operator. As she gave the message, it began, "Alfredo supped with Emily and me tonight." "Supped" read "slept" when the message was delivered, and on his return Dr. Perry facetiously challenged Alfredo, a music teacher at the academy, to a duel!

More and more of his close associates retired, and Perry was often called upon to speak at the ceremonies. At the retirement of his friend Endicott Peabody, for fifty-six years headmaster of Groton and certainly one of the "giants," Perry commented, "The headmaster's day is surely one of interruptions and decisions, decisions and interruptions, and when he goes to bed at night, if he has done half the things he intended to do on that particular day, he closes his eyes content."

Yet he never lost his sense of humor about the job. On return from an engagement at Deerfield, Perry wrote to Dr. Boyden, "I have seldom enjoyed a visit to Deerfield more. I think our evening was one of the best, mainly because you spoke. Juliette thinks that you and I are both comedians. Perhaps this is what we were made for after all, not schoolmasters."

Perry's concern for private schools was unceasing,

and he frequently saw to it that Exeter gave a hand to good institutions that were struggling to survive, as he had years earlier for Deerfield. In 1942 Perry wrote an article for the *Atlantic Monthly*, "Boyden of Deerfield," a fine tribute to his remarkable friend. He also served on the boards of a number of institutions, such as Deerfield, where he and Boyden were an unbeatable team; Miss Porter's in Farmington, where his daughter, Emily, was a student; Shady Hill, where Katherine Taylor was the director and which enriched Exeter with so many well-prepared students; the U.S. Naval Academy, where he never felt much at home; Thomas Edison's Talent Search Committee; and the Commonwealth Fund, Mr. Harkness's foundation, which gave so much so wisely to advance education and medicine.

Perry's interest in public education, on the other hand, was never as deep as it ought to have been. Through him the faculty knew something of the British public schools, the equivalent of our prep schools, but we learned nothing of the German *Gymnasium* or the Danish Folk High School. One exception to this deficiency was Perry's relationship with Arthur Barry, an Exeter alumnus and principal of Peabody High School. With several members of his faculty Barry would visit Exeter each year, and these meetings were welcomed by Exeter faculty as an opportunity to talk shop with their public school counterparts.

Throughout his career Perry was very proud that he had always run a democratic school, as opposed to other headmasters who ruled autocratically. At weekly faculty meetings he presided with great skill, often by word or gesture breaking a logjam that might otherwise have gone on for hours. He encouraged unity without unanimity. On one occasion, when he was outvoted by the faculty, he observed: "I had the comfortable assurance of being right which ought to have warned me that I was wrong."

An example of his letting the faculty lead was the fraternities matter, which climaxed in 1942. For years Perry had worried about these institutions, and it is characteristic of Exeter that under Perry's leadership a faculty committee recommended their abolition and that the act was completed not by ukase of the principal, but by vote of the faculty.

Such faculty integrity and independence were fundamental to Perry's vision of education. He never lost faith in the necessity for preserving academic freedom. When some of his friends sought his influence in ridding Williams College of Professors Max Lerner and Frederic Schuman, considered by some to be dangerously leftist, he defended the professors and even urged critics to attend their lectures.

He was never far from activity at Williams. When President Baxter wanted the trustees to allow him two days a week in Washington on government assignment, Perry supported him. "But they feel he ought to be in Williamstown, so, as usual, I am in the minority, but right."

Perry's last year as principal, 1945–1946, was in some respects difficult for him. He was sixty-nine years old, and he was tired. Yet in a way he *was* the academy. Anxious about the future and, of course, his successor, he watched with concern as Thomas S. Lamont, soon to succeed his father as president of the trustees, spent weeks on the campus, familiarizing himself with the school in preparation for his own duties. Several members of the faculty thought Lamont himself wished to be the ninth principal, even though he was also chairman of the search committee seeking to find Perry's successor. Perry did not need such worries, especially with the task of finding places on the faculty for the thirty-four men who had entered the service and were now returning.

What made the relationship with Thomas S. Lamont especially awkward was Perry's close friendship with Thomas W. Lamont, for so long president of the trustees. The two men shared similar backgrounds: both born in modest circumstances; both sons of preachers; both small-town boys. Unlike Lamont, Perry never wrote a book of reminiscences, but his letters reflect the same kind of family life in Williamstown as Lamont had had in the Hudson Valley. Perry's career as a college teacher and school principal may have lacked the glamour of the international banker's life, but both were men of the world. And Perry delighted in their common values when he urged Lamont to publish his book about his youth, *My Boyhood in a Parsonage.*

It was Lamont to whom Perry initially wrote about his retirement in a letter of April 20, 1945. It set a final date of June 1947, although if prewar teachers had returned by then, Perry hoped the date might be changed to June 1946. Lamont promised to bring the matter before the trustees.

Perry's opening talk to students in September 1945 was the last he would offer. He dictated it to his secretary, Elaine J. Ross, who worked for him in the thirties and forties and who would later serve two other principals and one acting principal. No doubt that day he thought back to the secretaries who had worked for him years before at Exeter, Katherine Julian and Ethel Mayo. Perry tended to dictate slowly; but he answered mail promptly, and he insisted on expensive stationery. Miss Ross composed many letters for his signature, but she could not always create the unique turn of phrase that characterized Perry's style.

In that final address Perry summarized the effects of the war, and his tone that day was as idealistic as the man himself. He concluded in a characteristic blaze of fervor:

> We can no longer doubt that freedom itself depends on responsibility, justice, and respect for the rights of all men everywhere. We must pledge ourselves solemnly to oppose an easy-going return to normalcy and a cowardly and provincial isolationism.

The complete address may be found in the Appendix.

On November 1, 1945, Perry wrote the inevitable letter to Thomas W. Lamont:

> As the war is over and as the fall of 1946 seems the natural time for my successor to take charge

of Exeter, I should like to retire as Principal of the Phillips Exeter Academy in June 1946.

No words of mine can express the feeling of appreciation to the Board of Trustees for their unfailing kindness and support. It is with real sadness that I tender my resignation.

In 1945–1946, the year I returned to the campus, the school seemed to run itself. Everyone wanted to make Perry's last year a happy one, and changes were assimilated comfortably. The ambitious new scholarship plan was inaugurated. A course in Russian language was offered. Prices continued to rise, and cost to the school per student became $1,700. Tuition, board, and lodging went up from $1,050 to $1,250. The Lewis Perry Music Fund was created. Yet enthusiasm for all new projects was tempered by the knowledge that of the 3,700 alumni who had been engaged in the war, 120 were killed and 11 remained missing in action.

That year we all felt ourselves part of history, looking backward and forward and reflecting on the paths the school had taken during Perry's tenure. When he had become principal in 1914, student enrollment had been 572; now there were 725. The faculty had numbered thirty-two; now it was eighty-two. In 1914 the campus had held twenty-nine buildings; now it contained sixty-two. The endowment had been $1,307,523; now it stood at $15,821,724.

This was a year for cherishing memories, for recapturing scenes that would never be played again. Once an alumnus walking to chapel just behind

Perry noticed that the principal kept looking back, first over his left shoulder, then over his right. The alumnus couldn't resist asking him why. "I just wanted to know where trouble might come from."

All of us remember Perry as a confirmed pipe smoker, although he surrendered the habit in his old age. Throughout his years as principal, however, he always delighted in a pipe, as his natural air of relaxation and *joie de vivre* was enhanced by his skill with the implement. It enabled him to think over a question and delay the answer.

Smoking was not usually permitted at faculty meetings in those days, but when the principal lit up his pipe, especially at end-of-term meetings, it was a signal that others were welcome to smoke. At such a moment Norman McKendrick, a history teacher, always drew out his handkerchief and covered his nose with it. When Perry and Dean Kerr were driven up High Street on their way out of town on their annual spring trip to the Bach Festival in Bethlehem, Pennsylvania, they always stopped smoking their pipes until they had passed the McKendrick house!

If Perry was at home with a pipe, he was a complete stranger to anything mechanical. His way at the wheel of a car was legendary. One Saturday night he drove Mrs. Perry to look in on a school dance. Satisfied that all was well, they returned to their car, but he could not start it and had to ask the night watchman to push him home. When the watchman tried to start the car, it turned over right away. "I know what the trouble was," said Perry. "Those young couples looked so happy I just forgot to turn the key."

On June 1, 1946, the academy celebrated Perry-Lamont Day. It was, needless to say, a very moving occasion. These two men had devoted a total of sixty-one years to the academy. Perry was completing his thirty-second year as principal, while Lamont, who had been graduated from Exeter in 1888, had been a trustee since 1917, and president of the trustees since 1935. Hundreds of alumni returned to Exeter from all over the country. A service of commemoration was held in honor of Exeter men who had lost their lives in World War II. The meeting of the General Alumni Association was held in Thompson Gymnasium and was addressed by Dr. Claude M. Fuess, headmaster of Andover; Oscar W. Huasserman, '08; Judge Charles W. Wyzanski, Jr., '23; Mr. Lamont; and Perry.

Some of the most moving words of the day were offered by Vernon Munroe, '92, an old and trusted friend of both Perry and Lamont:

> Their retirement means a great loss to the Academy for their places cannot be filled, but their successors can make places of their own as Dr. Perry did after Dr. Amen died. Many must then have thought Dr. Amen's place could not be filled. I do not call this the end of an era, for I doubt if eras ever really end. The ship is merely going about on a new tack, that's all.
>
> We owe these men our thanks, our gratitude, and "Godspeed." We shall owe their successors our loyal support.

During the spring of 1946 there had been some indication that the trustees might invite me to succeed

Dr. Perry. On one occasion I was coaching a crew from my single shell, several miles downriver, when a coaching launch came speeding down and the driver, Chan Sanborn, said I should get down to Boston to see some trustees as soon as possible. On this occasion in Boston, as in several other interviews with trustees in Exeter, much of the conversation dealt with faculty salaries and the possibility of a much expanded scholarship program. When the trustees met at the Exeter Inn in June, I was asked to be available at my home. Thomas S. Lamont, who had just succeeded his father as president of the trustees, walked to our house late in the evening, informed my wife and me that I had been elected, and escorted me back to the trustees' meeting. I accepted the appointment in spite of my reservations about leaving full-time classroom teaching and my doubts about the appointment of a current faculty member as principal.

Among the hundreds of letters of appreciation that came during Dr. Perry's last year, I shall quote from only one, from Professor John Finley, '21, of Harvard. His letter is the quintessence of the many. Here is the last paragraph:

> But the main thing is that you are what you are, the kindest, most generous, most amusing, wisest of men, and that being such, you have become a part of what is best in all the boys who have known you. It must be a very moving thought to you (though you doubtless never put it so yourself) that wherever these boys, most of them now men, show perspective, tolerance,

courage, and humor, there is something of you. How much more of you there must be in those of us who had the luck to know you well. If anyone should have the sense of a job well done, you should, and in the most inward, most important sense. For all this, it is impossible to give thanks enough, but I think you know what one would say.

At last the final day came: June 18, 1946, Dr. Perry's last Exeter commencement. In his farewell to the senior class he spoke of the need for personal development and for the continuance of the graduates' education. He recalled some of the history of the academy and in particular his debt to Dr. Amen.

Suddenly his tone grew wistful, and although we had so long denied it, we knew that at last the final moment had come:

And now a personal word. There are few people here this afternoon to whom I am not indebted. The parents for having faith in us, the friends for their interest in us, the faculty for years of cooperation and trust. I would like to speak of all of them, but I shall mention but two: Wells Kerr, our Dean, who for twenty years has taught the boys in school that they have a body of rights which would be respected, and who has given his decisions with absolute justice, unsuccessfully trying to conceal the affection he has for all of you. And Corning Benton, our Treasurer, who I think in the last twenty-five years has devoted more effective hours to the school and more thought to the school than any other one man. And there are many others to whom I am bound in affection and confidence.

I could never have done the job without Margaret and Juliette Perry, who have performed a miracle of affection and sympathetic confidence. Nor could I have done the job without my children, to whom the town and the school have been so kind. And to make the last weeks happy has come the election of my successor, William Gurdon Saltonstall, who has all the qualities needed to carry on the school we love. He will be called a great Principal and he will deserve the title, but in their heart of hearts William and Katharyn Saltonstall will know, as Lewis and Juliette Perry have known, that there is no such thing. They will know that the school is for all of you and they will thank God, as we do, for such understanding, such loyalty, and such affection.

Goodbye and God bless you, Classmates of 1946. You are now more than ever a part of all of this that we see, and the more precious part which is outside the range of vision, but not beyond the understanding of the faithful heart.

Lewis, Jr., drove his father home in the new car donated by the alumni. With the switch turned off, they sat quietly for a moment. Then Dr. Perry spoke. "Well, now Bill's principal."

HIS FAVORITE PLACES

IN HIS years of retirement Dr. Perry frequented two places he had enjoyed all his life: his home at West Chop, Martha's Vineyard, and the Tavern Club in Boston. Both were worlds apart from Exeter, yet to each Perry brought the same exuberance and capacity for joy that had made his life at Exeter so rich.

The community of West Chop was founded on a rainy day in April 1889 when three couples, Dr. and Mrs. John Homans, Mr. and Mrs. Charles Jackson, and Mr. and Mrs. Henry Greenough, came to the sandy tip of the island known as Martha's Vineyard with a view to making their summer homes there. Mrs. Samuel L. Fuller, author of *The Early Days of West Chop* and sister of Mrs. Greenough, described the event:

> Less fortunate than the spies of Canaan, they found a place flowing with neither milk nor honey, but through the mist and the rain they felt, rather than saw, the view from the cliffs, and here they decided to locate. The three men

were fortunate and distinguished, fortunate in the life work which they had chosen, and fortunate in their families. The three families were the Pilgrims of West Chop. They founded a less narrow, less laborious, possibly less significant but more cheerful Plymouth Colony.

Since then West Chop has remained a family community, with Perrys, Goffs, Pullings, Cruikshanks, Traffords, Grandins, Masons, Carters, Daltons, Badgers, Saltonstalls, Welds, Fullers, and others going back summer after summer.

In 1914 Lewis and Margaret had been passengers on the steamer from Woods Hole, which in those days landed at Harry Greenough's dock at West Chop. As soon as he stepped ashore, he looked around and vowed, "Here's where I want to spend my summers as long as I live." For fifty-one years he kept that vow! Perry was not a sailor, but he loved being on and in the warm waters of Vineyard Sound. And it was a rare summer when my wife and I failed to sail over to see the Perrys at their relaxed best.

Over the years at West Chop the Perrys enjoyed the company of Katharine Cornell, Thomas H. Benton, and that of a great many educators as well. The Perrys had a large, comfortable house in the woods, with a spacious porch and a view of Vineyard Sound. Their home was only a short walk from the Casino, the center of West Chop life with its tennis, dances, and Sunday services. With time Perry felt the need for a quiet workplace and hired a local carpenter to build "the shack," a small, one-room structure with a table, a couple of chairs, a couch, and a fireplace. When asked by the carpenter where to locate the structure, Perry pointed to a spot not far from the house, and there it still stands. The only trouble was that it was built on a neighbor's land, a small plot quickly purchased by the Perry family when they discovered the mistake. Perry's daughter, Emily, remembers that he often read aloud to her in the shack.

Perry became a focal figure at West Chop. He was a frequent tennis player with Jack Grandin, Storer Ware, Irving Badger, Harry Greenough, and, occasionally, Dwight Davis. Even when older, he retained the reflexes and skills to drop a towering lob on the baseline and send net-hungry opponents scampering back. He conducted Sunday services and hymn sings at the Casino, with Mrs. Susie Dalton at the piano, often using some of his favorite prayers and sermons borrowed from Ted Ferris, minister of Trinity Church in Boston. The Casino had dances on Saturday evenings, church on Sunday mornings, and tennis around the clock. The two criteria for admission for the seventy-five or so members were proximity and congeniality, and through all his years there Perry found just the kind of rest, good talk, reading, and stimulating company he needed.

Among Perry's wide circle of friends was Henry Beetle Hough of the *Vineyard Gazette*. In August 1957 Perry wrote Hough the kind of appreciative note he sent to hundreds of people:

> As always, I feel grateful that I have the privilege of reading *The Vineyard Gazette*. You

know better than I how good the paper is in its editorials and its news items. For instance, the last number with its account of John Mason Brown's lecture was extraordinary. I think I have never seen an account of a lecture which gave the lecturer's intent and phraseology so clearly expressed.

Recalling this letter in 1978, Mr. Hough commented:

It seems trite and superficial to speak of him as unpretentious, gracious, and friendly, but those were the genuine qualities I felt in him. He was more so than familiar phrases can convey.

As principal, Perry usually commuted between Exeter and West Chop rather than staying for the whole summer; but after his retirement the summers got longer, and he managed to keep in touch with fishermen and college presidents, doctors and businessmen, opera singers and headmasters. He especially enjoyed Sunday evening picnics at South Beach. The church services he conducted each Sunday at the Casino were short, fifteen minutes to a half hour, and well attended by all ages from one year up. A large overflow usually sat on the porch. Perry loved the place and the people and helped make the services a delight for his neighbors. He conducted his last one in 1951, talking informally about the early days in 1920.

For a man so fond of music, drama, and good fellowship, the Tavern Club in Boston was made to

order. Founded for the purpose of promoting literature, drama, music, science, art, and civic purposes, it
was Lewis Perry's favorite place. Perry tried to know
every member of the club, and among those he introduced were Wells Kerr, George Marshall, and Edward
Harkness.

As its president from 1935 to 1952 he was master of
ceremonies at luncheons and dinners, Christmas feasts
and serious discussions, clambakes and baseball
games. On trips to New York and back, his colleagues
at Exeter estimated that it took him about twenty-
four hours in Boston to get from North Station to
South Station. He almost always had to touch base at
the Tavern! His conscience pricked him a little about
being president of the Tavern Club because, as he said,
"It takes a great deal of time when I ought to be in
Exeter."

He was inaugurated as president of the club on
October 14, 1935. The following remarks on that oc-
casion were made by Claude Fuess, headmaster of
Phillips Academy, Andover:

> When the ordinary citizen thinks of a school-
> master if, indeed, he ever does, his memory turns
> to Arnold of Rugby or "flogging" Keate or Icha-
> bod Crane or some other classical specimen of
> austerity and aloofness. But Lewis Perry redeems
> his profession, by proving that it is possible for a
> headmaster to be human, to be amiable without
> condescension, witty without affectation, and
> convivial without shame. If Lewis were ship-
> wrecked, à la Enoch Arden, on a South Sea

island, he would lose no time in forming a club among the more fastidious and sophisticated savages, especially those who were willing to sit under the stars far into the tropical evening, drinking wine of coconuts and smoking furiously dried palm leaves. And it would not be long, I am sure, before they would be listening ecstatically to the dramatic tale of the Night Blooming Cereus.

Bliss Perry had been president of the Tavern Club in the twenties. Mark Howe, author of *The Presidential Range*, with verses for each president of the club, wrote:

> Two lovely Perrys on one stem
> (As Shakespeare nearly said it)
> Two jewels from the diadem
> That swells the Tavern's credit!
> But should a visitor from Mars
> Inquire, "Now who is Perry?"
> Together all the ursine stars
> Would sing, "It's Lewis Perry!"

His friends knew him as "the most famous toast-master of our generation" and praised his presence of mind and agility of speech. His introductions to the Tavern Club of men like James Bryant Conant, Harlow Shapley, Lord Halifax, Paul Robeson, Samuel Morison, and Hu Shih were models of brevity and warmth.

One Taverner recalled a conversation with Dr. Perry at Symphony Hall on a Friday afternoon:

They discussed a piece of music which Lewis kept referring to as "The Creation." Finally his neighbor in front (a lady) said, "Forgive me for correcting you, but the piece you are describing is *The Resurrection* and not *The Creation*." Lewis thanked her for the correction in his usual gracious manner. Just before Koussevitsky came to the podium, she turned again and said, "I hope you gentlemen don't mind my hat." Quick as lightning Lewis replied, "Certainly not, for that *is* a creation and not a resurrection."

On January 3, 1957, the Tavern Club held a dinner honoring Perry on his eightieth birthday. His music-maker friend Frank Hatch produced this ditty:

> Whom would I choose for boatman
> Across life's stream to ferry?
> Ted Ferris, Palfrey Perkins? No,
> Just give me Lewis Perry.

Cam Forbes sent eighty crimson roses, Perry's jovial and consummate leadership was celebrated, and all hands recalled the lively years of his presidency.

William James, who never could quite bring himself to finish his portrait of Lewis Perry because he so loved painting him and talking tennis and travel, said he could remember every former Tavern president—William Dean Howells, Henry Lee, Charles Eliot Norton, Henry Lee Higginson, Barrett Wendell, Bliss Perry, and Owen Wister:

> . . . each endowed with his particular personal distinction. Lewis Perry brought a magic

peculiar to himself. Men would arrive late in the afternoon, after their day's work, tired, and neither in love with the world nor even with their brothers of the Tavern. Then Lewis would beat on the table and begin to talk. The miracle then took place. Every man there began to love not only his neighbor but all other men. The tone of the gathering was transformed. Back of this, of course, was Lewis's inborn sense that all men are brothers. No other president of the Tavern, not even Lewis's superlative brother Bliss, was endowed with this gift.

Judge Perkins, another Taverner, was unable to get to Dr. Perry's eightieth party but wrote the following note:

> I want to go to the dinner because I have been to a great many dinners where you have presided, and each has been a tiding of great joy. We have laughed, laughed all together with utter delight, men of diverse ideas and temperaments and interests have laid aside all need of reticence and have been caught up in a wave of friendliness and warm companionship.

Lewis Perry loved clubs. And Bliss Perry's warning that he was too sociable was in vain. In addition to the Tavern, he belonged to the Class of 1898 Dining Club, the Burr Club, the Examiner Club, the Club of Odd Volumes, the Saturday Club, all in Boston, and the Century Association of New York. He loved them all,

but the Tavern, during his late years as principal and
the early years of his retirement, was his favorite. As
a member I was fortunate to watch his magic on
many occasions—his calling for order, "Taverners!
Taverners!!" several times before the talkative members would quiet down. Nothing upset him; everything about the club delighted him.

His most famous speech, welcoming new members,
is still read every year. His close friend Jimmy Otis,
after reading a copy of it that Perry had sent to him,
said:

> It will be popped into my locked tin box which
> contains, for meditation in my old age, only the
> most cherished communications. The quintes-
> sential spirit of the Tavern could never be better
> expressed than by your unique address. And no
> one but you could have written or spoken it. It is
> a genuine tour de force.

The complete speech is reprinted in the Appendix.
Here are the final lines:

> Perhaps you hear more truth spoken at the far
> ends of this table than in the immediate vicinity
> of the President, but Tavern truth is never bitter
> and always honest. I like to think of the two Tav-
> erners who were great men: William James and
> John Jay Chapman. They seldom agreed. No one
> could ever constantly agree with Jack Chapman.
> Once when Chapman had attacked William
> James furiously in a letter, James replied on a

post card, "You make me think of the Coroner's description of the corpse: 'pleasant looking and foaming at the mouth.' "

And so, as you take your places among us at this Christmas Feast, I can fairly promise you this: at the Tavern you will be surprised, amazed, bewildered, distressed, delighted, often incredulous, but never bored.

And how they loved it, and still love it! On his eightieth birthday, in a toast to Perry and his name, also that of a fermented beverage made from pears, the Taverners joyously raised their glasses:

Hail Lewis Perry! Hail! A grand name, Perry! A fermented drink, peerless Perry, fermented Perry, stand forth. Be steadfast. Keep the rules. (1) Don't do anything you don't want to. (2) Sit in a chaise longue by the Library fire. (3) a pipe in your mouth (4) *Pride and Prejudice* in your hands (5) a Siamese cat in your lap (6) a little blue flower in a glass beside you and (7) Praise God as we all do for giving you to us. Well done, good and faithful fermented Perry, beloved Perry—*Ubique, ab omnibus in saecula saeculorum.*

WEB OF FRIENDSHIP
1946–1970
✖❦✖

Almost seventy when he retired, Lewis Perry nevertheless continued to live a rich, active life. He never lost enthusiasm for people or for the other long-standing joys of his existence.

The Perrys moved to Boston in 1946 and lived for a short time on Beacon Hill in an apartment at 1 Acorn Street, close to their friends Mr. and Mrs. Philip Allen. They then moved to the Vendome, a hotel on Commonwealth Avenue, almost exactly midway between the Tavern Club and Symphony Hall. The geography was properly symbolic; Perry was poised between two of the pleasures he enjoyed most.

In the twenty-four years of his retirement Perry united all the threads of his life to form a single web of friendship. The giant exuberance of spirit that had always shone in the careers of all the Perry clan found in Lewis its foremost embodiment. A warm and caring human being who never took himself too seriously, his friends included United States Presidents as well as fishermen, authors and musicians, professors and opera singers, generals and admirals, football coaches and professional baseball players, scientists and columnists, governors and actors, college presidents and painters. The list was endless. Each friend was touched by his modesty and his genuine interest in people. One of them borrowed from Leigh Hunt a birthday verse which concluded:

> Say I'm weary, say I'm sad,
> Say that health and wealth have missed me,
> Say I'm growing old, but add
> Lewis kissed me.

Above all, Perry is remembered for his kindliness, his compassion, his caring for people of all sorts. He was patient with difficult parents when he was at Exeter, and that attitude carried over to anyone in trouble. Once, on a cold, windy day in November, when he was in his late eighties, he went out with his Scottish nurse, Isabel Gordon, for some fresh air and sat on a bench on the Commonwealth Avenue Mall. His good friend Erwin Canham, editor of the *Christian Science Monitor*, came walking by and urged the old gentleman to return to his apartment in the Vendome Hotel. "Oh, no, we can't go yet," answered Perry. "We're watching a man's coat." Then, from far down Commonwealth Avenue, came a man weaving up the mall. It was a wino who had been sitting with Lewis and the nurse on the park bench and had decided to buy them ice-cream cones. As he left, he had asked Perry to mind his coat, and Perry was doing just that. The wino approached naturally without the cones, and Perry, with great dignity, returned the coat. Only then did he and his nurse return to the Vendome.

Perry loved books and good talk more than ever. During much of his retirement he used the Boston Athenaeum as his library almost daily. Walter Muir Whitehill, then the Athenaeum's librarian, remembers:

> He developed the habit of spending many mornings there, regularly settling himself in a sunny alcove on the second floor, where he could smoke his pipe. He gave such an enchanting picture of a satisfied reader that it would have been worth my while to offer him a small honorarium to come and occupy that alcove.

Perry retained his concern about life at Exeter, an interest that I valued perhaps more than anyone else. A single sculler faces astern but can keep on course by aiming the stern of his shell at a mark on the shore behind him. Perry was that solid oak astern, who helped keep me on course during the long years of his retirement. Each September, as school was about to open, I would receive a note from him, wishing me luck at the first faculty meeting and expressing his hope and confidence that the school would have a good year. Never did he write a word of criticism. Invariably he found something encouraging to say.

Perry remained an avid fan of Exeter's teams for the rest of his life. A week before the 1948 Andover football game he wrote to Martin Souders, chairman of Exeter's Department of Physical Education, offering some amateur tactical advice:

> We'll give those Andover boys something to think about. Is Bill Clark playing from the T for-

mation now or the single wing? The T formation is wonderful if you have the men to do it, but not so good as the single wing for the average team.

I am sorry that Perce Rogers is going to resign as coach of the hockey team, but don't let Bill Saltonstall take over the job. He has enough to do without that. We'll lick Andover in hockey this year and then get some good intellectual who can coach hockey. We want some young ambitious fellow full of fire and with good judgment to take over the job.

Perry always felt at home with athletes. Each year after the World Series, Red Rolfe, '27, Yankee third baseman, would come to Exeter and give him a detailed firsthand account of the Series.

Perry maintained contact with many, many alumni. He worked on memorizing names; but he was never extraordinary in this respect, and although some thought he had a marvelous capacity, others judged him formal, even remote. Once, while he was dining at the Vendome, an alumnus paused at his table and identified himself as an Exonian. Perry half rose (a totally unnecessary response, but he was a man of great courtesy) and said, "Oh, yes, I remember you well. What is your name?" If he was sometimes bad at names, he carried the moments off in such a way that few people minded. And he often had friends at his side who would brief him on the name of an approaching student, alumnus, or parent.

Among the alumni with whom Perry corresponded was Tom Ragle, '45, now president of Marlboro Col-

lege, but in 1951 a newly appointed member of the
Exeter faculty. To him Perry wrote of his own educational philosophy:

> I find myself this week thinking of you a great
> deal as you start in your work at Exeter. I know
> you will be very successful and turn into an ex-
> cellent teacher. Sometimes it is not so important
> what you tell a class as to be the kind of man you
> want to be. I believe in education and always
> have, but I have noticed that those who educate
> best are those who share in their lives what edu-
> cation really is. This seems involved and perhaps
> sounds foolish, but I am sure there is something
> in it.

Though Perry was no longer on campus, the school
continued to benefit from his efforts. The $3 million
bequest of Dr. Arthur Elting, '90, came in 1948, but
Perry and Wells Kerr were in large part responsible
for it. Elting was an outstanding surgeon, a banker,
and a highly successful investor. He was also one of
the leading big-game hunters of the country, and his
collection of African animal heads, now housed in
Phillips Hall, has interested and sometimes angered
thousands of Exeter students.

If Perry had anything resembling a full-time occu-
pation during these years, it was as a speaker. He was
in constant demand, and he tried to fulfill as many
engagements as possible. One favorite place, of course,
was Williams. On October 12, 1946, Perry delivered
the address at the Williams College World War II
victory reunion. As a faculty son, as a former student

and professor, and as a trustee he was deeply moved by the occasion. Coincidentally, on October 17, 1919, Bliss had been the speaker at a Williams convocation after the First World War. Both meetings were held on beautiful autumn days in Williamstown. In his address Lewis Perry commemorated the 118 Williams alumni who had died and honored the 3,559 who were in uniform. "Read history," he said. "Be strong. Be patient. Have faith."

In July 1948 Perry gave an address on behalf of the fifty-year class, his Class of '98, at the Williams Alumni Association meeting:

> The last way we feel is anything which approaches a feeling on the melancholy side. What have we learned in fifty years? You can look at us and see that life has touched us. We know more than we did in 1898 what the world is made of, but as we talk together how much have we changed? We have lived through three wars, two of them catastrophic, we have all had sorrows and some disappointments, we have far more understanding of other people than we had fifty years ago; but to be perfectly honest, how much have we changed?

In 1953 Wells Kerr, appointed dean by Perry in 1930, reluctantly retired. At a tribute before the New York Alumni Association, Perry received a warm welcome but with characteristic modesty turned the applause to his old associate:

> It is heartwarming to be welcomed like this. The things you deserve the least are the things

you appreciate the most. I remember a new boy (it was his first day in school) who asked me a very difficult question. He came into the Principal's office, looked me over, and then said, "What do *you* do around here?"

Tonight we are honoring Wells Kerr who, in Exeter for thirty-two years, has done a difficult job supremely well. As I think of him there floats up a breath of life's morning that makes the world seem young and fresh once more.

From the first he has always guarded the body of rights which the boys in school have. He is *fair*, fair to the boys and fair to the members of the faculty. His decisions are never automatic; they come after a struggle and sometimes after sleepless nights, but they are always fair, for he has never played favorites.

Some of you, to use a euphemistic term dear to us at Exeter, may have been "separated" from the school by Dean Kerr. If you have been, I will guarantee that you are one of his greatest admirers. He has maintained noble social relations with his boys, in the belief that creeds are nothing, life is everything. He seems to say: "Know all you can, love all you can, do all you can—that is the whole duty of man."

Such a man never grows old. One of the things I miss most since I left Exeter is the visits I used to have with Wells in my office about five-thirty in the afternoon, after a day in which we had had a little of everything. A kind of academic sunset whose afterglow has never faded. Nor will the

afterglow fade after Wells has left Exeter, for of
him it can be said that "honor begets honor, trust
begets trust, faith begets faith, and hope is the
mainspring of life."

At graduation that June, as he left for the ceremonies, Perry asked Juliette what more he could say
about Wells Kerr. She shot back, "Tell them that
Wells is the perfect combination of Sherlock Holmes
and Elsa Maxwell!" I can still hear Perry's timely
pause, as listeners wondered who would be combined
with the great detective.

One place to which Perry always returned with
delight was Deerfield. In 1961 he served as master of
ceremonies at the commencement for the fortieth
time! Among his thoughts:

I was afraid I could not make it this year but
Dr. Boyden said that was ridiculous. This is a
very strong word for Dr. Boyden, so, for the
fortieth time I call the meeting to order. Deerfield, to me, is a miracle drug—one dose, and
from whatever ails you, you are cured! We used
to have rainy Commencement days in Exeter, but
by the time Frank Boyden arrived in the afternoon, the sun invariably was shining. And what
shall I more say?

Throughout these years Perry spoke to a wide variety of audiences, such as the Scotch-Irish Society of
Pennsylvania, the Boston Dental Improvement Society, the Society of New England, and at commence-
ments at such schools as Loomis, Groton, and Milton.

His best-known story—I heard him tell it a dozen times—relates his experience at Thomas Edison's house in 1927 which brought him together with Charles Lindbergh, recently returned from his great flight, George Eastman of Kodak fame, Henry Ford, and President Samuel Stratton of MIT. Mr. Edison had called the group together in West Orange, New Jersey, for the selection of a boy to become a student at the Edison laboratory and to be developed as a successor to the "electrical wizard." The story could not possibly be told in another person's words. The sound has been recorded, but the sight was just as important. The story took fifteen or twenty minutes to tell, with an audience steadily chuckling and frequently breaking out into roars of laughter. It told how Mrs. Edison had asked Perry to carry a night-blooming cereus late at night to the very deaf Mr. Edison's room so that he could see it. Dr. Perry never told the story the same way twice, and it seemed to improve with each retelling.

During the late 1940s and 1950s Perry was associated with the Boston Symphony Orchestra, first as a trustee from 1947 to 1954, then as trustee emeritus. Tanglewood was his special interest, and for more than ten years he served as chairman of the Friends of the Berkshire Music Festival. Among his many friends was Serge Koussevitsky, the conductor, and following his death the Perrys continued to see his widow, Olga. One snowy Friday Perry left the concert at the intermission to look for a cab, knowing it would be difficult for Mrs. Koussevitsky to get one after the concert. She wrote her thanks:

Dear Lewis:

Forgive the informality of addressing you by your first name. But I was so touched—as was Alice James—to learn that you missed the last part of the concert to secure a cab for us, that I want to say "thank you" from my very heart. A warm word is more than a cold medal! And so to you and Juliette goes my warmest affection, in the hope to see you both again before long.

During the 1950s and 1960s the Perrys became devoted members of Trinity Church in Boston, and Ted Ferris, the minister, became their very close friend. One Sunday morning the Perrys were walking home from church when Mrs. Perry suddenly accused her husband of having fallen asleep during the silent prayer. Perry denied the allegation and asked her what she had been doing during the prayer. Without hesitation she replied, "Oh, I thought of all the people to whom I forgot to send Christmas cards." When he conducted summer services at West Chop, Perry borrowed excerpts from Dr. Ferris's sermons and prayers.

Perry had always been somewhat perplexed by the biblical account in John 11:1–11, of Jesus's turning water into wine. One Sunday, when Dr. Ferris used this portion as the text for his sermon, Perry, who had never been told its meaning, thanked Ferris with the following note:

A little girl friend of mine who was six years old was sitting in front of the fire with her mother and father. She looked up and said to them, "Are you married?" Her mother said, "Why, of course." "Well," said the little girl, "nobody ever tells me anything."

That's the way I felt yesterday about the water and wine. It has always troubled me and seemed entirely out of keeping with what Jesus did usually. There was a little show-off quality to it, but you explained it wonderfully.

As Perry grew older, he naturally saw a lot of his doctor, Ben Ragle. Perry was overweight and had diabetes, shingles, and failing eyesight, but Dr. Ragle and later Drs. Arthur Pier, Richard Whiting, Maurice Fremont Smith, and Reed Harwood helped keep him in fairly good shape. No doctor ever denied him his whiskey and milk in the afternoons. Dr. Ragle closed a letter reporting on various tests by saying, "For an old sinner you are remarkable. Think fast, walk slow." Thus, Perry carried on, "not defying age but just passing him by with an indulgent chuckle."

Even about his physical ailments Perry maintained his humor. When an ear specialist treated him, Perry asked, "Can you make me deaf again? Juliette talks too much!"

If I had to choose one word to describe Perry, that might be "humane." And so it was most appropriate that an endowment was raised at Exeter to establish the Lewis Perry Professorship in the Humanities. On January 2, 1957, I sent him a letter on behalf of the trustees. It concluded as follows:

We only wish that you yourself might be the first occupant of the chair! Whoever holds it in the centuries to come, will bring to teaching and to the Academy more grace and sensitivity and humor because he gladly teaches in your name.

On the next day, January 3, Dr. Perry's eightieth birthday, the trustees formally saluted him:

Your school felicitates you, salutes you, embraces you. It is your school, for although you never went there, you came here, and you have made the school yours and it has made you ours.

For thirty-two years you led us, years of leadership which brought the school into leadership. One has only to compare the Exeter of 1914 with the Exeter of 1946 and of today to realize what your principalship meant and means.

Physically, you virtually recreated the Phillips Exeter Academy. First came the Thompson Gymnasium, Lamont Infirmary, Thompson Science Building, Wentworth, Amen, and Cilley, followed by the great burgeoning of the Harkness Plan, with Jeremiah Smith, Phillips, Bancroft, Wheelwright and Merrill, and the miraculous transformation of Abbot, Peabody, Soule, and Hoyt, and of the Academy Building itself—truly a physical refounding that in a few short years added more to the school's equipment than the preceding years had ever done.

Academically, you likewise virtually recreated the Academy. Through the princely generosity of Edward Harkness, engendered by his warm friendship for you, you were enabled to increase and enrich the faculty and institute an educational program without precedent or parallel in its potential for closeness of contact between teacher and taught. The wisdom you used in adding to the faculty is attested by the strength and standing of that faculty at the very forefront of American secondary education.

At the same time, in all the change and improvement, you held steadfast to the tested traditions of this school's long history—traditions of hard work, of sturdy independence, of democratic equality, of sound character.

Your thirty-two years here were good years, very good years—years of friendliness for boys and parents and faculty, years of commonsense leadership, years in which the world increasingly realized that Exeter is a great and fine school—a realization brought about, in large measure, because the world saw in you a great and fine Principal.

In happy recognition of all these blessings, we are honored to establish at Exeter

THE LEWIS PERRY PROFESSORSHIP IN THE HUMANITIES

Those who gladly teach in your name, for centuries to come, will be strengthened and gladdened by the example you set.

Exeter, New Hampshire

William G. Saltonstall Francis T. P. Plimpton
Principal President of the Trustees

The creation of the Lewis Perry Professorship gave the school an opportunity, eleven years after his retirement, to express its appreciation for his continuing interest in the affairs of the academy. Three years later, in acknowledgment of his constant support and encouragment of music, the school's new music building was named after him. In outdoor ceremonies the handsome building was dedicated, as the Academy Orchestra, Brass Ensemble, and Glee Club performed magnificently. In his speech Perry recalled the difficulties he had presented to his early piano teachers and reminded the large assembly, "A singing school is a good school." After the dedication he told me that there was no other building he would rather have named for him.

But as Perry grew older, sadness intruded inescapably into his life. In 1954, at the age of ninety-three, Bliss Perry died in Exeter. He and Lewis, oldest and youngest of the five brothers, were very close. They took trips abroad together. They shared a colorful correspondence. And they shared their profession as teachers of English and American literature. In 1960 Lewis wrote an article in tribute to his brother which was published in the November issue of the *Atlantic Monthly*, the magazine of which Bliss had been editor for some years.

In the late fifties Lewis, Jr., was divorced from Florrie Dalton Perry. Perry had known Florrie and her family for years and commented about this divorce to an old friend, "Don't think when you are eighty that you lose the power of being unhappy." In 1961 the final tragedy occurred when Juliette

Perry suffered a crippling stroke. Until her death four years later, Perry took most devoted care of her, with the help of "Cousin Bessie" Crocker. She was not only his contemporary, but she enjoyed the same things, recalled similar experiences, and made life warmer for him during the lonely years of Juliette's final illness.

On January 3, 1967, Perry's ninetieth birthday, mail arrived from faculty, alumni, and friends the world over. Wells Kerr wrote a long letter which is reprinted in its entirety:

Dear Dr. Perry,

A ninetieth birthday surely allows a man a fairly large degree of freedom to speak his feeling and thought about you. So on this occasion I should like to try to express the admiration and affection that so many feel for you. I like to recall you as you appeared at certain times and to mention some qualities that have been so much a part of your life.

You have been a great head of a great school. Taking over from Dr. Amen in 1914, you added a strength, a grace, and intellectual enlightenment that brought Exeter to a very high level. You developed a splendid quality of teaching, you made us all feel that we were part of a tremendous adventure. Educational theory, the kind that appears in gray educational journals, interested you little. Rather, the warm personal relationship between student and teacher was all important. You adopted as an article of faith the definition of another great teacher, a friend and admirer of you. "Teaching is the intimate engaging of personality with personality through the medium of some liberal thought by which the less mature of the two grows in stature of his humanity to the fullest height which is possible for him."

I like to think of you in your relations with people, with members of the faculty, with students. You couldn't always remember all the boys' names, but names or no names, you touched them with a power of your personality. Your trust in men who worked with you was so great that it established a loyalty, overreaching differences of opinion. That faith of yours in people somehow made them better than they might ordinarily be. Your humor reflected your delight in life. Some of my happiest recollections are of the late afternoon visits to your office when you would tell some humorous happenings of the day, always kindly, full of enjoyment of the incongruous.

I like to think of you in chapel conducting the morning service or perhaps reading Mark Twain's Sherburn-Boggs story, or Benét's *The Devil and Daniel Webster*, or Stephen Leacock's bank experience. Your most famous story, "The Night-blooming Cereus," never got to chapel. You established in the minds of boys the image of a high-minded, generous, understanding person, and that image had its powerful effect.

There is so much more that I could say. But on

this, your ninetieth birthday, the one important
matter is to express the love, the admiration that
I and thousands of others have for you, "forever
echoing in the heart and present in the memory."

Dean Kerr's letter may be said to embody the feelings of Perry's colleagues. One brief letter, by Thomas
Stephenson, '33, puts into a very few words what
thousands of alumni must have remembered:

Dear Dr. Perry,

The greatest satisfaction in life must be help-
ing others. I can attest that next to my parents,
Exeter under your leadership had the greatest
influence on my life. The "Mr. Chips" aspects of
your manner are legendary, but the substance
of your career is the quality of Exeter's faculty
and facilities.

I am grateful to you and Exeter for what you
taught me: the dignity of the individual, the purpose of study, the joy of life.

In 1967, at the age of ninety, it became necessary
for Perry to leave the Vendome. Even when well into
his eighties, he had always been able to come down
the hall to greet visitors at the elevator. But no longer.
Now he moved to a nursing home in Bryn Mawr,
Pennsylvania. His stepdaughter, Mrs. William Peltz
and his daughter, Emily Perry Cox, need not have
worried about informing him of the move. When told,
he seemed to welcome it. "Well, I guess I'll have to
become a Philadelphia gentleman instead of a Boston
gentleman."

Plans were made carefully for the long trip. Dr. Perry rode in an ambulance accompanied by Emily or Mag, who took turns driving a separate car. They all decided to make a spree out of the event and planned to stop for a picnic lunch along the road. They met at the place agreed on, opened up the window of the ambulance so the sun could pour in, and thoroughly enjoyed their martinis and sandwiches. Perry and the two women had a delightful time, and as they left for the remainder of the trip, he remarked, "Dear girls, we must do this more often." And so he moved into Bryn Mawr Terrace and Convalescent Center, where he received excellent care and was adored by both patients and nurses.

Had not extraordinary measures been taken by the doctors in Boston, he might have died of a serious illness two or three years earlier. But in his final years he continued to enrich the lives of others and to make light of his limitations. "How many men over ninety years of age," asks a close friend, "stricken with diabetes, unable to walk, assaulted by the indignity of catheters, not to mention other crushing disabilities, subjected to the lack of privacy of such establishments, could effortlessly win the affection and be the delight of the surrounding personnel?"

Two old friends from the Tavern Club, Peabody Gardner and George Weld, came down from Boston and formally presented him with a gold medal in honor of the fiftieth anniversary of his membership. Although he had not been able to stand for some time, he struggled to his feet and made a speech of acceptance. After these ceremonies Dr. Perry was seen in his pajamas, sitting on the edge of his bed with the ribboned medal around his neck. On another occasion, taken by wheelchair to a family wedding, he was heard by the congregation to inquire, "When are they going to serve the champagne?" Fermented Perry was living up to his name!

Isabel Gordon of Elgin, Scotland, for many years his nurse during his old age, reports in a letter of March 30, 1978:

> I still get a pang when passing The Vendome. Dr. Perry was a happy man in spite of the dreary interludes, diminishing senses, and mental faculties declining towards ultimate zero. Everybody loved him, and I felt very privileged to be with him so long. He was no problem to his doctors. He didn't suffer physically and loved to be read to which was a great pleasure to me since we both enjoyed the same kind of literature.

Perry became ninety-three years old on January 3, 1970. He died in Bryn Mawr some three weeks later on January 26, 1970. At a crowded memorial service in Trinity Church the Reverend Ferris touched just the right note. Perry in retirement had paid repeated tribute to Ferris, "who has done more for me than anyone." At the service Ferris reciprocated:

> Let us now in the presence of God remember Lewis Perry!

> We remember how he grew, naturally, steadily—like a tree—upward and outward; and how his roots went silently downward into the facts of

life, into the ground of existence; how he took the storms in his stride;

We remember how moveable he was, taking the changes of life without changing his course; he was never a stranger anywhere; and no one was ever a stranger in his presence.

We remember the things, places, and people he loved;

> the books he read,
> the music he heard,
> the school he made great,
> the clubs he enjoyed,
> the church he served,
> the men he taught—in school and out of school,
> his friends, his wife and children;

We remember the sound of his laughter, how cosmic it was;

> the roominess of his heart, closed
> to grievances and grudges, but
> open to people of every kind and variety;
> and the purity of his spirit,
> clear, clean, straight, transparent;

We thank thee, O God, for this good man; and when we remember him we cannot think that life is dull or that the world is a lost cause. A world in which Lewis Perry can grow and flourish as the green bay tree is thy world, O God, and to thy name be the praise, the honor, and the glory. Amen.

A summer graveside service was held in Williams-town, in the college cemetery, to the nearby sounds of undergraduate tennis, the game he played so well and loved so much. There, in a pine grove overlooking the Berkshires, Lewis rejoined his family.

A grandson of Thomas W. Lamont's looks back on Perry in these words:

> When I attended Exeter in the early forties I looked up to Lewis Perry almost as a pigmy views a giant: I was a shy and lowly student; he was a great man . . . it seemed to me he possessed those other endearing qualities that bring happiness to lives that are often humdrum. He was the most charming person that I had ever met, and my guess is many hundreds of people of all ages from all walks of life will agree with me. Many will describe his disposition as genial and cheerful, and indeed it was in my observation. He was a colorful personality.

His good friend and colleague Harris Thomas remarked:

> He guided the school through difficult times with grace and ease. He believed in people, he respected them as human beings, as individuals worthy of attention, and as personalities to be enjoyed. And he had educational ideals. He had for all his suavity and social grace a sense of the dynamic in life in people about him. This may have been so because he frequented in Boston, in New York, and elsewhere sophisticated friends of broad culture and with a sense of responsibility about the growth and welfare of the human race.

He brought to the Exeter scene an awareness of a rich and invigorating world, not hostile to but certainly strange in our hard-bitten New England.

At the Exeter faculty meeting on February 10, 1970, Arthur Landers, chairman of the Music Department, presented a minute on Lewis Perry. The complete text is reprinted in the Appendix. Here are its closing lines:

Throughout his full life, to use his own phrase, he was exploring "the possibilities of human beings for a larger and better life." Boys became better learners, men became better teachers, and boys and men became better persons for having known Lewis Perry.

Like his father, Lewis Perry was a "professor of life." He took life as a long-distance runner, not as a sprinter. His famous stories were not one-liners; rather he rambled unhurriedly into many a byway. His human warmth was combined with great dignity. And he was at home everywhere, not only in Williamstown, Exeter, Boston, and West Chop but in London, Paris, and New York.

Though our memories grow dimmer, we shall never forget the twinkle in his eye, his urbanity, his quick wit and contagious laugh, his buoyant optimism. He was indomitable in his old age and his capacity for the generous enjoyment of life was a lasting example to hundreds of teachers and thousands of boys.

APPENDIX

Words by and about Lewis Perry

❧⁂☙

I

ON June 21, 1920 Perry's leadership was recognized by Williams College, which awarded him the degree of Doctor of Humane Letters. He was to receive several such honors during his career, but his first, from his Alma Mater, was special. The citation read:

> Native and to the manner born, by right of descent, and loved by generations of Williams men, a true son of Ephraim, he is entitled to wear the royal color of his native hills and of his college. Not only with a sense of his worthiness but with real affection his Alma Mater confers upon him the purple robe of the humanities of which he has been so consistently an apostle and of which he himself is so worthy a representative.

II

THE complete text of the letter sent on October 30, 1930, from Lewis Perry to Edward Harkness, delineating what came to be known as the Harkness Plan.

My dear Mr. Harkness:

I have tried to make the letter definite. We want you to understand that if we receive this gift we are going into the plan wholeheartedly. It is a plan in which we believe and one which we think will be of primary importance to American Secondary Education. No school has ever had the chance for constructive work which will be ours if you will give us this grant.

1. *Size of sections.* Boys will be taught in sections of ten each, in any case not over ten. There might also be special sections of approximately ten boys or less containing

 (1) groups of those who have unusual difficulty with a particular subject;

 (2) groups of boys who should go ahead as rapidly as their ability will allow them.

It is also possible that a teacher may occasionally wish to assemble the boys in larger sections for purposes of a general talk, but this will be an extraordinary and unusual occasion which will seldom occur.

The English schools have succeeded quite remarkably in sectioning their boys according to attainment by individual instruction, by forma-

tion of special sections, by considering promotion
at odd times, and we should be able to accomplish
this through the use of small sections. By one
means or another the English do get the individual forward at a rate that has relation to his
powers. We believe that Exeter can also do this
and that other American schools will follow.

2. *All instruction will be carried on by the
Conference or Tutorial Method of Instruction.*
We plan to follow the conference or tutorial
method of instruction. What we have in mind by
the conference method, is the substitution of "serious consultation or discussion" for "the delivery
of something memorized."
The situation we picture would be:

(1) a conference room, equipped with books,
    pictures, and whatever else would be ap-
    propriate to the subject;

(2) small groups of students as nearly ho-
    mogeneous as such a large school would
    make possible, sitting around a table with
    a teacher with discernment, sympathy,
    background, and a live and full knowl-
    edge of his subject, who would guide and
    direct the discussion of the lesson. With
    the smaller groups and the conferences the
    teacher would see more completely the
    content and the processes of the student's
    mind. The greater class discussion inher-
    ent in the conference plan would train
    each boy gradually to learn to talk and to
    think while he is talking. The net result

would be that the boy would become more grown-up, would think of his studies as something more real, and would have an interest, a compelling motive, which he would carry to college. The successful teacher in the conference plan would be not a drill-master, but a partner in a human enterprise. We plan to supplement this by frequent conferences of the boys individually with their instructors, preferably in the instructor's study. Such conferences would be anything but formal instruction; rather talk about work and the boy's attitude to it and the direction of method of study.

3. *House System.* Another significant result from the addition of so many men on the faculty would be the revision of the proportion of instructors to boys in the various academy houses and dormitories. Great gain would be derived from the smaller number of boys under the charge of each instructor, approximately twelve. Careful study has shown that these smaller groups can be arranged in the existing academy houses and in new isolated apartment groups in our dormitories, and that the boys' residence commonly can be continuous in the same building for the last three years of his course. The four new dormitories will be built on this plan, preferably with dining rooms in each and our old dormitories adapted to this plan. Thus we hope to develop here something like the relation which ex-

ists between teachers and pupils in the English schools. The adoption of this system to our life and needs at Exeter would prepare boys for the house system in colleges.

4. We have already made arrangements to get Mr. Humby of Winchester College, England, to come over for the second half of the current year. Mr. Humby is one of the best science teachers in England. If this new plan goes through we would also try to get Mr. Ridley, who is a tutor at New College, Oxford. Mr. Ridley has already signified his desire to come. With these two men who are thoroughly conversant with the tutorial methods in England we would start on this plan with a great advantage. We plan to have two men of this sort for at least two years, and it is the desire of some of us that we may make a rather close connection with such a school as Winchester in order that we may find out more of their methods and their technique in teaching.

Although the Academy and its students would be primarily benefitted by all this, yet we believe the plan would be of great significance to American secondary education in general:

   (1) important conclusions will be reached regarding the effect of the relative size of sections on individuals;

   (2) the conference method of teaching will be here tried out under most favorable conditions;

   (3) the English sectioning of groups according

to abilities and attainments should show other schools how individuals can go forward at a rate that has relation to their powers, how boys who seem to have few intellectual interests, who are shy or who think they are dull, can be made to have an interest in their work;

(4) also Exeter could point the way for secondary school students to meet the conditions of college life in the tutorial and house systems by providing a sort of apprenticeship in school in some of their essential features.

Our aim would be to cooperate closely with tutorial systems in the larger universities eventually hoping to approximate the English method of having individual boys assigned to University tutors while they are still in school.

Needless to say, the success of the plan would depend most on the quality of the men secured for the positions, but the reputation of the school, and the possibility of participation in this plan, would draw men of the right calibre and spirit. They, too, will bring ideas, and thus there will be created a center for experimentation and guidance in American secondary education that would always continue.

5. The estimates of cost which follow are final and the school will stand back of them. Those for new buildings have been gone over with great care and are based on unit costs of buildings erected before the present drop in building prices,

which of course may be only temporary, and we should hope to save something on these figures, especially if building costs remain at approximately the present level.

I hope this letter is clear and definite enough for your purposes. In an enterprise of this kind, which involves very complete changes in present methods of teaching, it is difficult to state definitely in advance every detail of such a program, but the main principles which are stated here have been very carefully considered by some of the ablest men in our faculty, by Mr. Jeremiah Smith, Jr., the President of our Board, and by all of our trustees, and have been unanimously approved by them, and I am sure there is no difference of opinion as to what we are all aiming at.

> Sincerely yours,
> Lewis Perry

III

PERRY's opening address to students in September 1945, the beginning of his final year as principal.

THE YOUNG MAN IN A NEW WORLD

It is a great pleasure to welcome the school this morning, at the beginning of our one hundred and sixty-fifth year. Particularly, I want to welcome the new boys who are here with us for the first time. We can all feel that it has taken the work of a great many different people to get us all in our places this morning.

The new boys do not know exactly what kind of school this is. It certainly differs from most schools. We believe that the age of responsibility can be brought down for American boys and, therefore, we have as few rules as possible.

You will find that your advisors will do everything possible for you—get to know your advisors at once. And this is important: *speak to the other boys in school* whether you know them or not.

If you have read the E Book, and I hope you have, you will know that at Exeter work comes first. From a comparatively long experience I know that the work here in Exeter is not too hard for the average boy and that the work is stimulating for the boy who is above average in his studies.

I want to welcome the new members of the Faculty who join us for the first time. They, too, may not know at first the particular flavor of Exeter. I hope that our particular teaching flavor here will give them pleasure in their teaching and a wide scope for all their powers.

Last year I said that we were opening in what I considered the most critical year in American history. It turned out to be an amazing year, an unbelievable year. Exeter was founded, as you may know, in 1781, before the War of the Revolution was over, and we have always been American to the core of us.

For four years we have been sending our teachers and our alumni into the great fight for freedom. Many teachers and over thirty-five hundred of our alumni have fought for our cause. Well over one hundred of our alumni have given their lives for us.

And, now, thank God! Peace has come and we dare look back and see with clear eyes how we were feeling on the opening days of the last three years. Even we civilians have been through a great deal!

In 1940 France had fallen. Belgium was overrun, England was open to her enemies. The Battle of Britain had not been fought. At that time, 1940, Winston Churchill said: "You ask, what is our policy? I will say—it is to wage war, by sea, land, and air, with all our might and with all the strength God can give us: to wage war against a monstrous tyranny, never surpassed in the dark, lamentable catalogue of human crime. That is our policy. You ask, what is our aim? I can answer in one word: Victory." And it sounded like empty rhetoric.

By the time the school opened in *1941* we were the arsenal. There was tremendous production. England was being bombed almost beyond endurance. Many of us were worried because of the power and numbers of the isolationists in this country. The opening in 1941 was a low period in our spirits. Some of our boys had begun to get into the services. Our seniors will remember.

1942 was for most of us an exciting time, a

time of great activity. England, we thought, would never be invaded, but the bombing continued. Pearl Harbor had united the country. Most of our boys of suitable age had enlisted. Our thoughts were on Africa and the Mediterranean. Our spirits were lifting.

1943—Great talk about a second front. The news from the Pacific, which had been bad—many said that we were losing the war in the Pacific—was getting better and we were landing our Marines, who, with great courage and great losses, were capturing beachheads and moving inland. Our Navy was magnificent and so were our men in the air. On opening day, 1943, every one of us had had friends killed. The country was empty of young men over eighteen years of age.

1944—Last year D-Day had come and gone. We were winning victories on the Continent. We suffered from a false optimism about the end of the war with Germany. A miracle had been performed and we expected greater miracles. But most of us felt that the war with Japan would drag on for a long time.

1945—V-J Day proclaimed by the President, a day of thanks to God. Some of our boys back, others coming. The fears about those we love, on the whole, not realized. Happy people on a blessed spot on the happiest opening for a dozen years. We are appalled by the tasks ahead, but what we faced bravely in '40, '41, '42, '43, and '44 we can still face bravely. We have all played our roles, some great, some small. Our Exeter boys in the services have played the greatest roles of all, and as the curtain goes up on the next great act in the history of the world, let us, like Solomon, pray for wisdom. Courage—yes, endurance —yes, perhaps we have these qualities now, but we have not proved as yet that we have those rarer qualities—the wisdom and the intelligence to make this a fairer world for our grandchildren and their children.

We do not yet know what war memorial we shall have at Exeter for those of our sons who have given their lives so that we may live in freedom, but what more practical and lasting memorial can there be than scholarships for boys who otherwise could not have the chance for an education such as Exeter affords. The effort to put such scholarships in the right hands will be one of the most interesting and, I believe, most worthwhile of our undertakings this year.

Among the most pleasant experiences of the last few months at Exeter have been the visits of old boys who have been in the armed services. The things which they have to tell us about what they have been doing make us feel proud of them, and also very humble. One thing that stands out is the number of these boys with distinguished records in the Army and Navy whom we remember as former scholarship boys, fellows who earned their way through the Academy by hard work and high marks. There have been exceptions both ways, but mostly it seems that the boys who made the most of their opportunities in school have made the best of conditions as they found them in the services. One cannot help a feeling of pride when every now and then one of these fellows says, "I could never have got where I did, if it hadn't been for Exeter." You can't dispute evidence of this sort, even if you wanted to.

Those of you who have read Mr. Cowles' article in the last *Bulletin* know already that one of our greatest fears is that Exeter should be regarded as a rich boys' school. It has never been one and it never will be. From the first day of its founding, the primary purpose of the Academy has been to provide an opportunity for any worthy boy to get an education, no matter how little money he may have. No one must be allowed to think otherwise.

Committees of the Faculty and of the Trustees worked last year on the problem of scholarships and in the spring their recommendations were adopted.

Because it was evident that if we wanted more needy and deserving boys at Exeter someone must go in search of them, a new administrative position was created, that of Director of Scholarship Boys. The man who will fill this position is H. Hamilton Bissell, himself a former scholarship boy at Exeter and for the twelve years since his graduation from Harvard a member of the English Department here.

This is one patriotic contribution we can make for our country. I hope we shall make many others. We have reached the time in our civiliza-

tion of the atomic bomb. We have seen the sur-
render of Japan. We now face peace, bringing
with it the threat of normalcy when the echoes
of the bomb blasts fade. We can no longer doubt
that freedom itself depends upon responsibility,
justice and respect for the rights of all men everywhere. We must pledge ourselves solemnly to
oppose an easy-going return to normalcy and a
cowardly and provincial isolationism.

A great military victory has come to us and
our allies. There is no time, however, for us to
sit back in half darkened cathedrals and listen
to the well-loved chords of "Pomp and Circum-
stance." Our place is in the streets of the world,
sharing with mankind the hopes of a better day
and working for that end.

IV

On June 16, 1946, Perry participated in his last Exeter commencement. Here is the complete text of his
farewell to the seniors:

Classmates:

I am an honorary member of the class of 1884,
but Paul Carlson has made me a real member of
the class of 1946, a difference of sixty-two years.
I am one of those boys I have talked about to your
parents so much—a slow developer.

Just a few words before you go, and this year I want to say a few words to everybody else. But it won't be long.

We must not let this be a sad occasion. You boys have graduated from the Academy in two, three, or four years. It has taken me thirty-two, and I hope you feel as I do, that our education is by no means completed.

What we have been aiming at is *development*. You as a class are much stronger than you were two years ago. I could point to twenty men in this class who are twice the men they were two years ago. If you have come to the end without this development, then Exeter has failed. This development has come through two things, which I think we have to a greater degree than almost any other school in the world—*democracy*, which to us means that every . . . boy in school is judged for what he is. Every boy in school starts from scratch. I think that this has been true. And *freedom*, which to us means that you stand on your own feet, make your own decisions and grow into manhood as a responsible member of society.

This method has its disappointments and there is some wastage. Some boys drop out who might graduate in a more closely guarded school, but I would back this class against any other class graduating this spring from any other school in America. You are men, not boys. You have initiative, judgment, and that quality which is rarer than you know, whether in college or in the

services or in the world—*character*. How trite
it seems to say it, but this is the bedrock truth.

When I came here, in 1914, I was asked by
some newspaper to state what my policy was in
regard to Exeter, and I said that I had no policy
but that while I was in Exeter I should try to do
one thing—to tell the boys the truth. If I have
done that, I am content. And you young men
will be content, if you will stick to that. You will
be tempted to cut corners, to prevaricate; you
will be tempted not to face things and tell the
weakening white lies. I am not worried about
your scholarship, though some colleges this
spring suddenly seem to be; my great interest is
in how you are going to stand up, how you are
going to keep your friends, and how you are going to show moral courage when there will be the
temptation to side-step. Your parents have this
temptation, but they have gone farther up the
road than you, and have learned from experience.
But you and your parents can help each other for,
if there is absolute honesty at home, you need not
worry much about your honesty abroad.

My predecessor, Dr. Amen, was an absolutely
honest man; every one of us who knows the modern Exeter is under debt to him, who wore himself out because he could not tolerate sham.

And now a personal word. There are few people here this afternoon to whom I am not indebted. The parents for having faith in us, the
friends for their interest in us, the faculty for
years of cooperation and trust. I would like to

speak of all of them, but I shall mention but two: Wells Kerr, our Dean, who for twenty years has taught the boys in school that they have a body of rights which would be respected, and who has given his decisions with absolute justice, unsuccessfully trying to conceal the affection he has for all of you. And Corning Benton, our Treasurer, who I think in the last twenty-five years has devoted more effective hours to the school and more thought to the school than any other one man. And there are many others to whom I am bound in affection and confidence.

I could never have done the job without Margaret and Juliette Perry, who have performed a miracle of affection and sympathetic confidence. Nor could I have done the job without my children, to whom the town and the school have been so kind. And to make the last weeks happy has come the election of my successor, William Gurdon Saltonstall, who has all the qualities needed to carry on the school we love. He will be called a great Principal and he will deserve the title, but in their heart of hearts William and Katharyn Saltonstall will know, as Lewis and Juliette Perry have known, that there is no such thing. They will know that the school is for all of you and they will thank God, as we do, for such understanding, such loyalty, and such affection.

Goodbye and God bless you, Classmates of 1946. You are now more than ever a part of all of this that we see, and the more precious part

which is outside the range of vision, but not beyond the understanding of the faithful heart.

V

On March 21, 1946, three months before their retirement, Juliette and Lewis Perry were given a dinner
by the faculty. Myron Williams, director of studies,
offered this tribute, *The Man from Western Massachusetts.*

I have been amusing myself thinking of the
spring in Exeter thirty-four years ago. That was
in 1914. It was mud-time. The ice was all out of
the river. Fields were too soft and wet for baseball. Board walks were being taken up, to dis-
close galosh buckles and other treasures beneath.
Receding snow revealed on the lawns old bones,
orange peels, pop bottles. Spring was here "with
all her vernal garbage," as Corning Benton has
said so beautifully. It was just as it is now. Also,
just like this year, the great question was, "Who
will be the new Principal?" Fears, hopes, and
misgivings blew about in the meadow gales of
spring that year.

But things also were different in 1914. Exeter
had defeated Andover in football 59–0, and proceeded to win all other athletic contests. Tad
Jones was coaching football; George Connors,

track; and John Carney, baseball. The Infirmary
was a one-family wooden house; and the Graduate's House, also a wooden dwelling, "accom-
modated the guests of the school," to use a professional term. The real centre of Academy life was
the Third Academy Building on the site of the
present one and, directly behind it, the old gymnasium, with its imposing entrance. Behind Ab-
bott, and its mountainous heaps of coal—stood the
boiler plant. More than half of the 572 students
lived, not in dormitories, but in the houses of
townspeople. Things *were* different. But the
greatest difference of all was the darkness then
before the dawn.

Then the name of Professor Perry of Williams
College was introduced. Who was he? He might
be a great scholar but it would be a pity if ris-
ing academic standards should nip the series of
athletic victories just beginning. He was reported
to be young, handsome, a great tennis player,
and an enthusiast for the threatre. Academic
standards shivered. Fears, hopes, and misgivings
blew in through dormitories and dining halls.
Members of the faculty here tonight doubtless recall those confidential discussions, those conjec-
tures.

Well, now they know. And they know and we
know the difference which Lewis Perry's being
here for the past thirty-two years has meant to
the Phillips Exeter Academy—and to Dr. Perry
and Mrs. Perry. After all that has been said here
tonight, and all that has appeared in the press of

the country for the past few months, the only things left for a speaker in my place on the program to say about Lewis Perry, I am afraid, are things that won't bear repetition . . . not in his presence.

But this may be one way to do it. Some years ago you may remember a musical comedy called *Louisiana Purchase* appeared, a satire of the Huey Long administration. To avoid a libel suit, the management had printed on the program, "The scene of this play is laid in a fictitious country called 'Louisiana.' " This device enabled the authors to describe things as they were in Louisiana, even if the play should be given in New Orleans, itself. So if, in the course of my remarks, I should refer to a character whom I shall call Lewis Perry, I shall trust you do not draw hasty conclusions.

You have all heard the story of the traveller whom Dr. Perry picked up on the turnpike a few years ago, and who, hearing an attendant at a filling station address him as "Doctor," concluded, no doubt from the character of their conversation thus far—that he was a veterinary. I think strangers *are* often puzzled to place him. Boston? New York? Chicago? Harvard? Yale? Princeton? As a matter of fact, I know of scarcely anyone else who can feel at home anywhere sooner—and actually *begin welcoming the natives*, whether in Boston, New York, London, Martha's Vineyard, or Center Barnstead, New Hampshire.

The secret is that he was born and brought up
in a small town. Somehow it is not so easy to get
over being born in Boston or New York. But it is
a great advantage for a citizen of the world, as
Dr. Perry is, to have been brought up in a small
town. It gives a kind of guarantee of authenticity
wherever you go—like the accidental orange
seed in a jar of marmalade, or the tang of peat
smoke in a Harris tweed. Williamstown in Western Massachusetts is a great town to come from.
One can talk as safely about Western Massachusetts as about Louisiana.

Your Western Massachusetts man is not quite
like any other American, except a New Hampshire man, and that for somewhat the same reasons. He looks very much like the shrewd and
cautious Vermonter, to whom he is closely re-
lated. But he has turned his back on the Green
Mountains and, perched comfortably on the
Berkshire Hills, faces south and suns himself.
From here he looks with toleration over the rest
of Massachusetts toward Boston, and without
envy, down toward New York. . . . Hostility
rather amuses him. He appreciates the good
things of life, but he does not squander them. He
lives on a high plane, but his head is not in the
clouds. The Berkshire Hills are not high enough
for that. He sends his sons over to Williams or
Amherst to college; his daughters, to Smith or
Mt. Holyoke. He goes to the Congregational
Church. Above all, he minds his own business;
and his neighbors mind theirs. They don't hire

help so often as turn to and help one another,
swapping jobs and doubling up. Each man jack
is respected for what he can do. Leisure is, after
all, idleness; and the leisure class is regarded as
slightly feeble-minded. It is all what one finds in
any pioneer or frontier town; each individual
voluntarily doing what he is best adapted to do,
making a place for himself because his particular
skill is needed.

I am not pretending that Dr. Perry embodies
all the characteristics in Western Massachusetts,
or that he imported them when he came to Exeter. Many of them he found already here, and
these he encouraged. But some of these things he
certainly did bring. Let me read a passage from
his address to the Senior Class in June 1915:

"Beware of some of these fatal phrases of college life, such as 'When in Rome, do as the Romans do.' Think twice before you do as the
Romans do in Rome. . . . Do not be too much
impressed with the so-called 'big men' of the
undergraduate life, and do not set great store
upon the fact that you may be called a big man.
The significant thing is not always the prominent
thing, and the significant person is quite likely to
be the person who has no prominence at all.
There is a certain glory in a college career; it is
this, contrary to most endeavors in the world, in
college it does not pay to advertise."

It seems to me that the disappearance of the
old style "big man" at Exeter during Dr. Perry's
time is not wholly a coincidence. In his place has

come the well-rounded and competent young man, an exponent of true democracy in education.

In short, for the past thirty-two years, Exeter has been feeling the fortunate effects of the greatest civilizing influence in American history—that of the New England college in a small town. At the beginning of the last century, when men whose names are great in American history were young, the great universities were also small colleges in homogeneous communities. This is not an argument for the small college as against the large college today. The changing world may have changed us too. Only I say, that in Dr. Perry we have had the great leadership from the small New England college, to which we owe more than we may be aware.

VI

HERE is his famous speech, the president's address to new members of the Tavern Club.

We welcome you tonight into the friendship of the Tavern. I should be the last to define a good Taverner. The mold was broken before the Tavern Club was formed. But the best Taverners are those who are like no one else. We have no type, which makes the work of the Elections Committee difficult.

How were you elected? Ah, how were any of us
elected? Better men than we have been turned
down. We seem to have got along very well without standards. Our artistic, spiritual, and social
demands seem to be summed up in one Eighteenth Century epitaph:

"Blond, passionate, and deeply religious, she
was second cousin to the Earl of Leitrum and of
such are the Kingdom of Heaven."

Anyone reading the funeral oration of Pericles
must be struck by two things. He has little to say
of the possessions of Athens nor of its resources
for peace or war, but only of its people; and his
praise of the people is praise not of the things
they can do but of the things in which they believe, the things to which their minds and spirits
attach.

Like all who have become members in the last
forty years, you are entering the Club at a time
when we are at a low ebb. We can only say that
we like you and hope that you will like us. We
are an association of gentlemen who know when
to unbend. Why haven't we been changed beyond repair by war and economic upheaval?
Probably because of good fellowship and friendship, sympathy in love of beauty in art and literature and character. A good club "softens the
ferocious, gives countenance to the meek and
comfort to the solitary, educates the over-learned,
and has been known to arrest the predestined
prig on his downward path."

When you enter the library downstairs, you

enter a room half filled with friends. If there are people whom you avoid, you are no Taverner. Our friendships in that back room stretch far into the past and they look into the future. There is a haunted mellowness, the ghostly bouquet of a thousand friendly conversations; and beneath the noise and banter and laughter we feel at home.

At the Golden Jubilee of Queen Victoria, the English Bench brought in an embossed scroll which began with the words: "Conscious as we are of our defects—"

"No, no!" interrupted Lord Mellish. "Let us not tell her Majesty a lie! Conscious as we are of one another's defects."

What are we now? We are a club which differs from other clubs in its intimacy. We are a group probably of over-contented individuals whose charm, and we modestly admit we have it as a club, is in the differences which constitute our intimacies. Our closest friends are those with whose opinions we do not agree, whose prejudices we do not share, whose conversation we cannot understand. We are individualists of so marked a character that if we are told we are individualists, we would deny the appellation in fifty different ways. Not that it is not true, but that we could not bear missing the fun of discussing it.

For we are a club of conversationalists—and what surprising and unprovable things we say! Here everyone has the right—it is almost a duty— to say things that he half believes to people who half understand. Here we can talk freely and foolishly because we like each other and we are never judged by what we say. We are serious men but in the Tavern we give ourselves a moratorium from logic, and we are not given to vote taking.

Perhaps you hear more truth spoken at the far ends of this table than in the immediate vicinity of the President, but Tavern truth is never bitter and always honest. I like to think of the two Taverners who were great men: William James and John Jay Chapman. They seldom agreed. No one could ever constantly agree with Jack Chapman. Once when Chapman had attacked William James furiously in a letter, James replied on a post card, "You make me think of the Coroner's description of the corpse: 'pleasant looking and foaming at the mouth.' "

And so, as you take your places among us at this Christmas Feast, I can fairly promise you this: at the Tavern you will be surprised, amazed, bewildered, distressed, delighted, often incredulous, but never bored.

VII

ARTHUR LANDERS, chairman of the Music Department, presented the following minute on Lewis Perry at an Exeter faculty meeting on February 10, 1970:

Lewis Perry, who died on January 26, 1970 at the age of ninety-three, was for thirty-two years Principal of the Phillips Exeter Academy. A member of a family distinguished in education and in the world of letters, he began his illustrious career as educator soon after graduation from Williams College in 1898. In 1914 he left the position of Professor of English Literature at his alma mater to accept the challenge of Exeter. He arrived here to find not only that the school was in financial difficulty but that its main building had been destroyed by fire. His wise leadership enlisted the cooperation of students, alumni, and faculty and inspired the confidence of such friends as Thomas W. Lamont and Edward S. Harkness. He guided Exeter through two world wars and a depression and, upon retirement in 1946, left the Academy in good health and in a position of pre-eminence. His legacy is all about us—in the Harkness classrooms and in the buildings bearing the names of Thompson, Lamont and Lewis Perry.

It is not as the nationally known educator—holder of five honorary degrees, friend and patron of music, member of learned councils and advisor to philanthropic organizations—that the faculty best remembers Lewis Perry. The new teacher or student meeting him for the first time received a firm handshake, a hearty "Glad to see you!" and what was probably the warmest smile he had ever seen. In Dr. Perry one felt he had

found a friend who understood his feelings, a
man he could count on. On closer acquaintance,
he learned that Lewis Perry had a passion for ex-
cellence, and that underneath the geniality and
gentleness was a persistent firmness and a confidence in enduring values. But he was always
approachable, always natural, always sympathetic.

He brought to faculty meetings, which he always conducted in the spirit of democracy, the
qualities of tolerance, understanding, and humor. A master story-teller, he knew how to re-
lieve tension and to focus the issue with a well-
told anecdote. He loved laughter, and if a joke
were on himself he enjoyed it to the full. When
he delegated authority, he made one proud to be
so trusted. He made men feel that what went on
in the classroom, dormitory or gymnasium was
something that mattered a great deal.

No one who heard his morning chapel services
will ever forget the deep, rich voice, the dramatic
pauses with which he read from the Scripture,
talked about current events, or, on certain occasions, read from Mark Twain, Stephen Leacock,
or James Thurber. It was as host at One Abbot
Place, however, that he most fully revealed the
magic of his charm, the genial courtesy, the taste
and dignity of a gentleman who genuinely liked
people, knew that life was good, and wanted to
make it still better. Years after they had left
school, former students flocked to alumni meet-

ings when they heard Dr. Perry was to be present, in order to enjoy once more the atmosphere of good feelings he always created.

Happily the years were kind to Dr. Perry. The man who had been a fine athlete in his younger days still took a lively interest in Exeter sports results as well as in all other Academy activities to the time of his death. The visitor who called on him at the Hotel Vendome in Boston when his ninetieth birthday was approaching was gladdened to find again the same serenity and warm smile. The fine voice greeted him with the assurance that Lewis Perry was glad to see him and genuinely interested to know how things were going.

Throughout his full life, to use his own phrase, he was exploring "the possibilities of human beings for a larger and better life." Boys became better learners, men became better teachers, and boys and men became better persons for having known Lewis Perry.

WILLIAM G. SALTONSTALL was the ninth principal of Exeter, 1946–1963. He taught at William Penn Charter School, at Exeter, and at Old Rochester Regional High School. He served in the U.S. Naval Reserve, the Job Corps, and was Director of the Peace Corps in Nigeria. He was also Curator of the Alfred North Whitehead Fellowship Program at Harvard's Graduate School of Education, Chairman of the Massachusetts Board of Education, member of the Board of Overseers at Harvard, and trustee of several schools and colleges.

The author of a maritime history of New Hampshire, he lives in Marion, Massachusetts, on the edge of Buzzards Bay, and enjoys sailing his yawl, *Arbella*, seven or eight months of the year. He is the father of five and grandfather of sixteen, and his two first loves are his family and the sea.